JUPITER

NEPTUNE

SATURN

PLUTO

ERIS

URANUS

Jeopardy! champion and *New York Times* bestselling author

KEN JENNINGS'
JUNIOR GENIUS
GUIDES

OUTER SPACE

BY **KEN JENNINGS**

ILLUSTRATED BY **MIKE LOWERY**

SEMPER QUAERENS

LITTLE SIMON
New York London Toronto Sydney New Delhi

THE OFFICIAL
JUNIOR GENIUS CIPHER

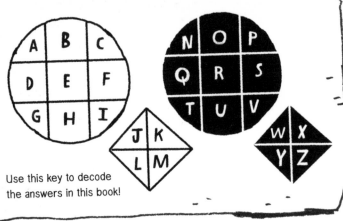

Use this key to decode
the answers in this book!

LITTLE SIMON

An imprint of Simon & Schuster Children's Publishing Division
1230 Avenue of the Americas, New York, New York 10020
First Little Simon edition October 2014
Text copyright © 2014 by Ken Jennings • Illustrations copyright © 2014 by Simon & Schuster, Inc.
All rights reserved, including the right of reproduction in whole or in part in any form. • LITTLE SIMON
is a registered trademark of Simon & Schuster, Inc., and associated colophon is a trademark of Simon &
Schuster, Inc. • For information about special discounts for bulk purchases, please contact Simon & Schuster
Special Sales at 1-866-506-1949 or business@simonandschuster.com. • The Simon & Schuster Speakers
Bureau can bring authors to your live event. For more information or to book an event contact the Simon &
Schuster Speakers Bureau at 1-866-248-3049 or visit our website at www.simonspeakers.com.
Designed by Elizabeth Doyle
Manufactured in China 0714 SCP
2 4 6 8 10 9 7 5 3 1
Library of Congress Cataloging-in-Publication Data
Jennings, Ken, 1974– author. Outer space / by Ken Jennings ; illustrated by Mike Lowery. — First edition.
pages cm. — (Ken Jennings' junior genius guides) Summary: "Now you can become a junior genius with
Ken Jennings' first children's series! With this book you'll become an expert and wow your friends and
teachers with out-of-this-world facts: Did you know that Mars has a volcano bigger than the state of
Arizona? Or that there's a star with a diamond the size of our moon at its core? With great illustrations,
cool trivia, and fun quizzes to test your knowledge, this guide will have you on your way to whiz-kid status
in no time!"— Provided by publisher. Includes bibliographical references and index. 1. Outer space—
Juvenile literature. 2. Solar system—Juvenile literature. I. Lowery, Mike, 1980- illustrator. II. Title.
QB602.J46 2015 523—dc23 2013042287
ISBN 978-1-4814-0171-5 (hc) ISBN 978-1-4814-0170-8 (pbk) ISBN 978-1-4814-0172-2 (eBook)

CONTENTS

INTRODUCTION

Good morning, my young friends! I'm Professor Jennings, a certified expert on everything and, luckily for you, your personal guide on your journey to becoming a Junior Genius. Everyone can become a Junior Genius, if they're interested in the world around them. *Semper quaerens*, that's our motto. "Always curious."

If you're like me (and, obviously, you at least *wish* you were) you sometimes look up at the night sky and ponder the mysteries of the cosmos. How did the universe begin? Is there life on other planets? What lies in the dark heart of our galaxy? How do people go to the bathroom in space? Today we're going to tackle those very questions by peering into the farthest reaches of outer space. The only telescopes you will need are my nearly limitless knowledge and your own imagination.

At the beginning of every Junior Genius book, we recommit ourselves to the pursuit of knowledge by saying the Junior Genius Pledge. Please rise, face this drawing of Albert Einstein, and place your right index finger to your temple. Repeat after me:

With all my fellow Junior Geniuses, I solemnly pledge to quest after questions, to angle for answers, to seek out, and to soak up. I will hunger and thirst for knowledge my whole life through, and I dedicate my discoveries to all humankind, with trivia not for just us but for all.

We're headed for space, Junior Geniuses. T-minus one page. Prepare for liftoff.

FIRST PERIOD

Our Mr. Sun

Have you ever complained about the Sun, Junior Geniuses?

"It's too hot today!"

"Ugh, that's bright."

"No more sunscreen, Mom!"

Well, after today's lesson, I never want to hear you bad-mouth the Sun again! The only reason that life can exist on Earth at all, everything from figs to walruses to TV repairmen, is because of the light and warmth we get from our nearest star.

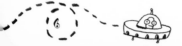

million years—that's "soon" in cosmic terms!) the middle of the disk got hot enough to light its nuclear furnace. The Sun was born!

A lot of the leftover dust and gas spinning around the new baby Sun began to clump together, which is how planets form. But these weren't the planets we know today! There were probably hundreds of little planets zooming around and smashing into each other, until they merged into bigger ones. Others collided at such high speeds due to the immense gravity of big planets like Jupiter and Saturn) that they shattered into tiny chunks called asteroids.

Today, just eight main planets survive, most of which are named for different gods of Roman mythology.

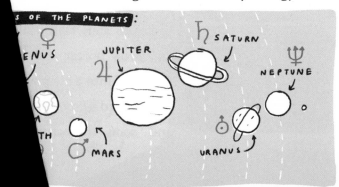

This is the Sun.

Wait, that's not right. Why would the Sun need to wear sunglasses? Think about it; how would that help? Let's try that again.

No Crayons Allowed

Please don't color this drawing with a yellow crayon, Junior Geniuses. Not only would that deface this fine book, it would also be *scientifically inaccurate*! Sunlight only looks yellow to us because we're seeing it through our atmosphere. From space the Sun is perfectly white!

When you look at the Sun—wait, hold on. Public service announcement:

The light is so intense it can literally cook the retinas in your eyes. To observe the Sun, glance and then look away. Don't stare. There are health faddists called "sungazers" who claim they get all their nutrition from staring at the Sun a few minutes a day. But that really doesn't work, so please don't try this.

Okay. When you *briefly glance* at the Sun, you're actually looking back in time! Sunlight travels at the speed of light, which means it takes an average of eight minutes and twenty seconds for it to reach the Earth. So the Sun outside your window isn't actually where you think it is. By the time you see it, the real Sun has moved forward two Sun-diameters in the sky.

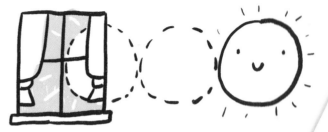

But we're going to travel back in time even fur[ther,] not eight and a half minutes but 4.5 *billion years!* when the story of our solar system begins.

A Star Is Born

Over 4 billion *nebula*—a gigan[tic...] of gas—colla[psed,] possibly due [...] from a ne[...] As it shr[ank, it] began [...] and [...] flat[...] t[...] a[...]

Pop Quiz!

Since classical times, we've used special symbols to refer to the planets and most refer to mythology. The Venus symbol, ♀, looks like a mirror, because she was the goddess of beauty. Mars looks like a spear and shield, ♂, because he was the god of war. What is the Neptune symbol, ♆, supposed to be?

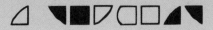

Spaceballs

But that diagram isn't *quite* accurate, because the solar system is much, much bigger than we can draw in a book. The Sun is *massively* bigger than everything else, for one thing. It accounts for 99.8 percent of the mass of the solar system! (Jupiter is most of the rest.)

The distances between planets are even harder to imagine. Let's pretend that a superpowerful alien has somehow shrunk the eight planets of our solar system to fit inside a baseball stadium. (This alien is apparently a big baseball fan.) The solar system is so big that our massive Sun would be the size

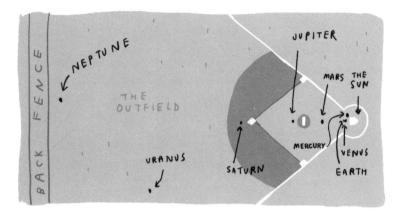

of a golf ball, sitting at home plate! At this scale, Mercury is a dust speck in the batter's box, while Venus and Earth are grains of sand near the edge of the home plate circle. Mars is another dust speck one-third of the way to the pitcher's mound. Jupiter and Saturn are the sizes of apple seeds, with Jupiter sitting just past the pitcher's mound and Saturn at second base. Uranus is a pinhead near one of the foul poles, and Neptune is a pinhead at the fence in deep center field. (Pluto got kicked out of the ballpark in 2006 for arguing with the umpires. Hit the showers, Pluto.)

Here's the bottom line, Junior Geniuses: Space is incredibly big. Our little solar system by itself—our own tiny neighborhood in a vast galaxy—is so big that it fries even my amazing brain when I try to think about it.

Junior Genius Joviality!

Ask a grown-up how far it's possible to see on a clear day. I guarantee they will guess low! The correct answer, as long as you can see the Sun, is "93 million miles." That's also known as one "astronomical unit"—the distance from the Earth to the Sun.

Whirled News

Today we take it for granted that the planets of the solar system spin around the Sun, but for most of history people have assumed that the Earth was the center of the universe! Five hundred years ago *heliocentrism* ("hee-lee-oh-SENT-rizz-um"), or the idea that the Sun was the center of things, was so controversial that people who believed it could be put on trial. The great astronomer Galileo spent the last ten years of his life under house arrest for insisting it was the Earth that moved around the Sun, not the other way around.

But—sorry, Galileo!—that doesn't mean the Sun is the exact center of the solar system! Gravity works both ways, Junior Geniuses. The Sun tugs on each planet—take Jupiter for instance—in a big way, because the sun is so massive. But, at the same time, Jupiter is tugging on the Sun in a small way. Instead of saying that Jupiter orbits the Sun, it's more

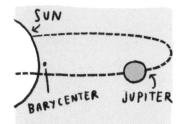

accurate to say that they *both* orbit a third point, called a *barycenter*, which is about thirty thousand miles above the surface of the Sun.

Are You Sitting Still?

The Earth is moving at a pretty good clip right now: spinning on its axis at 1,000 miles per hour and whirling around the Sun at 66,000 miles per hour. But don't forget that the Sun is moving too, spinning around the Milky Way like a giant pinwheel at about 483,000 miles per hour. And today scientists can use leftover radiation from the Big Bang to measure how fast our whole galaxy is moving through the universe: 1.3 *million* miles per hour!

We don't feel any of this motion, of course, because everything around us is moving at the exact same speed we are. But the next time a grown-up says, "Have you been sitting in that chair all day? Get up and get some exercise!" tell them you've already covered a few million miles today, and you're *pooped*!

All Systems Glow

But let's take a close-up look at the Sun. **(NOTE: AGAIN, DO NOT TAKE A *REAL* CLOSE-UP LOOK AT THE SUN. IT IS VERY BRIGHT.)** Luckily, Mr. Sun produces a lot of energy, or we would be very cold right now and bumping into things all the time. But where does that energy come from?

At the middle of the Sun is a very dense core, where the pressure gets pretty intense—over one hundred times what it is at the bottom of Earth's oceans, in fact. All that gravity pushes atoms together with a pressure of one hundred tons per square inch, enough

to crush atoms into each other. Hydrogen atoms fuse together to form helium atoms, and that process produces the energy that powers the Sun.

Lighter than Air

Helium is the second most common element in the universe (after hydrogen), but it went undiscovered until 1868, when astronomers spotted the wavelength of a new element in the sunlight emitting from an eclipse. Earth has large underground deposits of helium gas, but the element was discovered millions of miles away on the Sun almost thirty years before it was discovered right here under our feet!

The fusion in the Sun's core produces little energy particles called *photons*—but they don't radiate out into space right away. In fact, they bounce around inside the Sun for thousands of years before making their way to the surface.

So the sunlight you see in the sky today might have been born in the Sun's core as much as 170,000 years ago!

All that fusion produces a *lot* of energy. In fact, the Sun produces the equivalent of 77 trillion atomic bombs—*every second*. If we could somehow collect just one second's worth of that energy, it could power human civilization for the next half a million years!

Despite all that, the weird thing about the surface of the Sun is that it's not very hot. Well, okay, it's almost ten thousand degrees Fahrenheit, which is pretty hot for, say, a bowl of ramen. But it's not that hot on a cosmic scale. Right here on Earth, a bolt of lightning is five times hotter than the surface of the Sun, which doesn't seem right. The temperature at the core of the sun is 27 million degrees Fahrenheit, while its outermost layer, the corona, is 3.5 million degrees Fahrenheit. So why is the bright photosphere so much chillier than the dark corona?

For many years scientists were baffled, but a new discovery may partly explain the problem. We now know that, believe it or not, there are thousands of giant magnetic tornadoes swirling around the upper levels of the Sun at speeds greater than six thousand miles an hour. Some are the size of the United States! These twisters pull heat from the inner layers of the Sun and inject it out into the corona.

Fun on the Sun

Giant megatornadoes aren't the only thing the surface of the Sun has going for it. In fact, there's a lot to see on the Sun. **(NOTE: AGAIN, DO NOT TRY TO SEE THINGS ON THE SUN. IT IS DANGEROUSLY BIG AND SHINY.)**

DO NOT LOOK AT THE SUN!

SOLAR PROMINENCES

What are they? Huge loops of gas that surge out into space and can hang around for weeks or even months.

Cool, but why should I care? Because they're huge! The biggest ones on record extended half a million miles into space.

SUNSPOTS

What are they? Dark, cool dots on the Sun's surface caused by magnetism. They come and go in an eleven-year cycle.

Cool, but why should I care? They may have helped cause an ice age! In the late seventeenth century, a period of low sunspot activity called the Maunder Minimum corresponded with a period of bitterly cold weather.

SOLAR WIND

What is it? A constant stream of invisible but electrically charged particles the Sun releases in all directions.

Cool, but why should I care? It could interrupt your cartoons. Strong solar wind can mess up radio and TV signals. It also causes the auroras that shine in the sky over the North and South Poles.

SOLAR FLARES

What are they? Sudden bright flashes on the Sun that eject a massive amount of energy from the corona.

Cool, but why should I care? They could literally light you on fire! The Carrington Event was a massive solar storm caused by a flare on September 1, 1859. The northern lights extended all the way south to the Caribbean that day, and were so bright you could read by them all night. Birds started chirping at midnight, and people accidentally got up and went to work. Telegraph poles all over the world sparked, and some telegraph machines built up so much charge they could send messages without being plugged in! In Washington, DC, an arc of fire jumped from the telegraph to the head of its operator, badly burning him.

YAWN

It Came from the Oort Cloud!

The solar wind is also what puts the tails on comets! Comets are chunks of ice and dust a few miles wide that come from two areas with funny names *way* out at the edge of the solar system: the Kuiper Belt and the Oort cloud. Their very long orbits occasionally bring them near the Earth, and we can see their 60-million-mile-long tails of gas and dust being "blown" away from the coma (the "head" of the comet) by the solar wind.

COMA

TAIL

THE TAIL DOESN'T TRAVEL "BEHIND" THE COMET AS IT MOVES . . . IT ALWAYS POINTS AWAY FROM THE SUN.

Five Cool Comets to Know

SHOEMAKER-LEVY 9. Crashed into Jupiter in 1994, leaving scars that were visible from Earth for months.

SWIFT-TUTTLE. Causes an amazing meteor shower called the Perseids in the night sky every August as Earth passes through its debris trail.

THE COMET THAT KILLED THE DINOSAURS. Sixty-six million years ago *something* crashed into a shallow sea off the coast of Mexico, kicking up dust that killed 70 percent of all the species on Earth. Today many scientists believe the extinction bomb was a comet.

WILD 2. Visited in 2004 by a NASA probe called *Stardust*, which collected dust samples from its coma and shot them back to Earth in a little capsule for analysis.

HALLEY'S COMET. Swings by Earth every seventy-five years, so we'll see it next in 2061. The writer Mark Twain was born in 1835, when Halley's Comet was in the sky, and said he expected to go out with it as well. Sure enough, he died in 1910, one day after the comet's return.

Panic in the Streets

When Halley's Comet passed by Earth in 1910, one astronomer predicted that the gases in the comet's tail might be poisonous. The public freaked out, and crooked businessmen made a killing selling gas masks, "comet-proof umbrellas," and "anti-comet pills" that cost a dollar a pop!

Fade to Black

The Sun won't burn forever, of course. At some point it'll run out of hydrogen to fuse, and the lights will go out. That collapse will happen in about 8 billion years—but look at the bright side, Junior Geniuses. **It will finally be safe to look at the Sun without a grown-up nagging you!**

But before it gets colder, the Sun will do something worse: It will get hotter! In about 3.5 billion years, the seas will boil, and Earth will become unable to support life. Hopefully the human race will have found someplace

SECOND PERIOD

Lunar Learning

On July 20, 1969, 600 million people were glued to their TV screens, at the time the largest live television audience ever. They were watching grainy black-and-white footage of two men climbing *very slowly* down a ladder. It doesn't sound like great TV, but it was one of the most important moments in history. For the first time, a human being was about to set foot on the surface of another celestial body: Earth's Moon.

NEIL ARMSTRONG

Two American astronauts, Neil Armstrong and Buzz Aldrin, had descended from lunar orbit in a small space capsule called the *Eagle*. The automatic pilot was heading for a boulder-filled crater, so Armstrong had to take the controls and land manually. When the *Eagle* touched down on the Moon's Sea of Tranquility, the astronauts had only twenty-five seconds of fuel left!

BUZZ ALDRIN

Extra Credit

Edwin Aldrin got his famous nickname, "Buzz," as a child, when his older sister had a hard time pronouncing the word "brother." In a funny coincidence, his mother's name was Marion Moon!

It's easy to forget how risky the *Apollo 11* mission was, Junior Geniuses. By today's standards, the Apollo program's technology was amazingly crude. The *Eagle*'s computer was about as powerful as a modern digital watch. The total computing power of Mission Control, in Houston, was no greater than one of today's laptops. The astronauts navigated using paper maps, and when a circuit breaker snapped off during the landing, Buzz Aldrin fixed it by jamming a ball-point pen into the switch! The White House was well aware that the Moon landing had no guarantee of success and had prepared a gloomy second speech for the president to read if the astronauts were lost in space.

But the mission *was* a success! Armstrong's boots landed on the dusty lunar surface, and he said

Listeners on Earth didn't actually hear him say the word "a," either due to static or to Armstrong messing up his lines. So the quote didn't make much sense, but everyone got the idea.

When Worlds Collide

For centuries, people had looked up at the Moon, the brightest object in the night sky, and dreamed of visiting it. In the mid-1600s the French author Cyrano de Bergerac wrote about a voyage to the Moon, which he imagined was full of four-legged "beast-men." Way back in 1865 Jules Verne's book *From the Earth to the Moon* cleverly predicted an American Moon rocket launching from Florida—but in Verne's book the rocket is fired out of a giant cannon!

Extra Credit

NASA launches spacecraft from sunny Florida because the Earth rotates faster when you're closer to the Equator, giving rockets a little extra boost on their way. The Vehicle Assembly Building at the Kennedy Space Center, where rockets get put together, is the world's largest one-story building. The VAB is so huge that it has its own weather, including rain clouds that can form indoors!

But the Moon has been in our skies a lot longer than that. More than 4 billion years ago, scientists believe, a Mars-size "protoplanet" called Theia smashed into the infant Earth. Huge molten chunks of both planets flew into orbit. Within a matter of months or years, all this debris had coalesced into a single moon.

The Incredible Shrinking Moon

If you had a time machine that could take you back billions of years to see the newborn Moon, you'd notice one thing right away: It would be enormous in the sky! The Moon probably first formed just fifteen thousand miles from the Earth. That's only a few Earth radiuses away.

Today the Moon is about fifteen times farther from us: 240,000 miles, more or less, and getting farther away every day. Yes, the Moon recedes from Earth about an inch and a half every year, roughly a quarter the speed your hair grows.

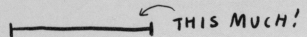 THIS MUCH!

Crater Face

Most things in the sky look more or less the same every day. **(Even the Sun, but just to review, don't look directly at it!)** The Moon is more like us: a little bit different every day.

Sometimes it looks like this:

The darkish patches are called *maria* ("MAR-yuh") from the Greek for "seas." The Sea of Tranquility that *Apollo 11* landed in wasn't an actual sea, just a dark plain formed by an ancient lava flow. Looking at the pattern of the dark maria and lighter-colored highlands, many people see a face—you know, the "Man in the Moon." But other cultures, like the Chinese and Aztecs, saw a rabbit instead.

Other times, the Moon looks like this, or this

depending on the angle the Sun is shining at. The Moon, of course, produces no light itself. It only appears to glow when sunlight reflects off it.

The line on the Moon between sunlight and shadow is called the *terminator*. Earth has one too, of course, dividing day and night. On Earth the terminator moves across the Equator at about one thousand miles per hour, faster than a commercial jet. But on the Moon the terminator glides along at a leisurely ten miles per hour. A man on a bicycle could keep up!

Pop Quiz!

What ocean phenomenon here on Earth is mostly a result of the Moon's gravitational pull?

Let's Get Together

On much rarer occasions, the Moon looks like this:

LUNAR ECLIPSE

SOLAR ECLIPSE

or this:

There are two types of eclipses. In a lunar eclipse the Earth passes directly between the Sun and the Moon. (It doesn't even say "Excuse me." How rude.) So what we see in the sky is the shadow of the Earth moving across the Moon. So if you wave at just the right time, you might be able to see your own shadow! (Not really.)

Solar eclipses happen more often, but each one is visible only from a small part of the Earth. In a solar eclipse the Moon passes directly between the Earth and the Sun. **(Junior Geniuses, do I really have to remind you again not to look at this?)** That halo around the Moon is the Sun's fiery corona, the only time it's ever visible.

Look! Up in the Sky!

The Sun and the Moon overlap precisely during a total solar eclipse—which is a complete coincidence. There's no astronomical reason why they should look the same size from Earth. The Sun just happens to be four hundred times bigger than the Moon, and four hundred times farther away. In hundreds of millions of years, when the Moon has drifted a few thousand miles farther from Earth, eclipses will no longer look so pretty.

Astronomers love eclipses because they give them a chance to see and study the outer atmosphere of the Sun. But other people can get scared when it suddenly gets dark in the middle of the day! Here are three eclipses that made history.

MAY 28, 585 BC. The Medes were fighting the Lydians at Halys, in modern-day Turkey. When the eclipse started, both armies took it as a bad omen from the gods and canceled the battle! Thanks to the convenient eclipse, this battle is the oldest event in human history whose exact date we know.

MARCH 1, 1504. Christopher Columbus was stranded in Jamaica, and the natives were getting fed up

with his crew. Consulting an almanac, Columbus learned that a lunar eclipse was coming, and told the tribe that he would darken the Moon if they didn't provide him with the supplies he needed. As you can imagine, when the Moon actually did start to darken, right on schedule, the locals *freaked out*.

MAY 29, 1919. Scientists photographed this eclipse to see if starlight was actually bending around the Sun, as Einstein's theory of relativity predicted. It turned out it was, which provided the first proof that Einstein was right.

Extra Credit

Have you ever heard the expression "once in a blue moon"? The Moon may look reddish during a lunar eclipse, or when it's low in the sky, but it never really turns blue. A "blue moon" is an old expression for an extra full moon in some calendar period, like when there happen to be two full moons in a month, or four in one season of the year. Today it can refer to any rare event— so when a grown-up says you only clean your room or brush your teeth once in a blue moon . . . um, it's not a compliment.

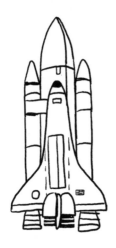

A Voyage to the Moon

It's been decades since the Apollo program was shut down, spelling the end of manned exploration of the Moon. For now, the only way to be a human being on the vast, airless surface of the Moon is in our imaginations. Here's what you need to know to visualize life on Luna.

It's Hot. Also Cold. Without any real atmosphere, weather on the Moon depends only on whether the Sun is shining. When it's sunny, it gets up to 253 degrees Fahrenheit, hotter than boiling water. When it's dark, it can get down to a chilly -387 degrees Fahrenheit! (By the way, there's no such thing as a permanently "dark side of the Moon." The same far side of the Moon is always pointing away from Earth, true. But sunlight moves across the whole lunar surface—except maybe in some shadowy craters at the lunar poles.)

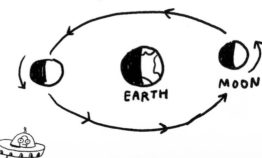

EARTH   MOON

You Won't Need an Ice Machine. Those dark spots at the Moon's south pole may be the coldest place in the solar system. Astronomers estimate that temperatures in these craters stay about four hundred degrees below zero *all the time*, which is probably colder even than Pluto gets. And probes have found evidence that these chilly craters are full of precious, life-giving water—frozen as ice, of course.

You Weigh as Much as a Bowling Ball. The Moon is much smaller than the Earth, which means its gravity is weaker. So everything on the Moon weighs just one-sixth what it does here on Earth. Even in a big, heavy space suit, you could jump twenty-two feet in the air. Alan Shepard, the astronaut who commanded *Apollo 14*, hit two golf balls on the Moon. He joked that the second shot went for miles and miles.

It's Really Dusty. The soil of the Moon's surface doesn't get eroded by wind and water, so each grain of dust is really, really pointy. Astronauts found that moondust could eat through three layers of the bulletproof Kevlar in their boots! It also makes dust storms in space capsules, static-clings to everything, and even causes hay fever.

You Can't See Your House. The Earth is visible in the Moon's sky just as the Moon is in the Earth's sky. It even goes through the same phases: a full Earth, a crescent Earth, and so on. It's four times bigger—about the diameter of a jam jar lid held at arm's length—but that's still not very big. A common myth says that the Great Wall of China is visible from the Moon. But astronauts have found that the Great Wall of China is almost

impossible to see even from a low-Earth orbit. (It's long, but very skinny and brown, so it blends right in.) From the Moon, all you can see of the Earth is vague swirls of blue and brown and white.

Bird's-Eye View

There are plenty of other interesting things you can see from orbit, however. Gordon Cooper, one of the Mercury astronauts, said he could even make out big trucks moving down a highway! Here are some other weird things to keep an eye out for the next time you're on the International Space Station.

• Cities, airports, dams, bridges, and harbors (especially at night, when they're lit up)

• Penguin poop (the reddish-brown droppings stain ice in Antarctica)

• A Saudi billionaire's name (Sheikh Hamad carved his name in half-mile-tall letters on his island)

• A beaver dam (the world's largest, in Alberta, is 2,800 feet across!)

• Pollution (oil spills, sewage, and wildfire smoke have all been spotted, unfortunately)

• A giant chessboard (in Germany, 1,200 feet across)

Someday humans will return to the Moon. You're younger than I am, Junior Geniuses. Who knows? You might just grow up to be the astronauts who do it. Recent NASA photographs reveal that all but one of the U.S. flags planted on the surface are still standing. But you'll notice one big difference, if you ever get to visit them! Over the past forty years, the harsh lunar sunlight has bleached them all completely white.

RECESS

I'm afraid astronauts don't get recess, Junior Geniuses. Their schedules are so crowded that their only free time is called *pre-sleep*: a couple of hours at the end of the day when they prepare and eat dinner and then get themselves cleaned up before bed.

They do have periods set aside for exercise. A couple hours on the workout machine is the best way to keep bone and muscle mass healthy in microgravity. And sometimes there's even time for sports. In 2011 Japanese astronaut Satoshi Furukawa sent a video to Earth demonstrating the one-man game of baseball he liked to play aboard the International Space Station. He would pitch the ball to the opposite end of his module, then float ahead of it, pick up a bat, and hit his own pitch. Then he'd dive ahead of the ball in order to field his pop fly. Talk about slow-pitch!

Solo baseball won't work under normal Earth gravitational conditions, so try one of these out-of-this-world games instead.

HULA HOOP

KICKBALL

Ring around the Saturn

You'll need a kickball-size ball for this one, and a hula hoop. Place the ball on the ground, stand about ten feet away, and take turns trying to toss the hoop over the ball. Each successful toss is a point, but you lose a point for knocking Saturn "out of its orbit" (making the ball roll so it comes to a stop outside the hoop). Game is to six points, since Saturn is the sixth planet from the Sun.

Comet Tag

One player starts out as the head of a comet. He or she is "it" and tries to tag the other players. Everyone who

gets tagged is pulled into the comet's gravity field and joins the tail of the comet by linking arms with "it" (or the previous player tagged). The last meteor floating free in space, untagged by the giant comet, is the winner!

Don't Planet Out

It helps to have a mnemonic ("neh-MAH-nick") device to remember things. For example, the planets of the solar system. For years there were nine planets, and students used sentences like "**M**other **v**ery **e**arnestly **m**ade **j**elly **s**andwiches **u**nder **n**o **p**rotest" to remember their order. (The first letter of each word is the first letter of each planet.)

But now that Pluto is off the official list, we need a new mnemonic! In this game everyone sits in a circle with a piece of paper and a pencil. Write the letters *MVEMJSUN* down the left side of the paper. Everyone starts their sentence with an *M* word and passes it to their right. The next player must think of a good *V* word for the new paper and pass it on. When everyone has written the last word, read the sentences out loud. They might be something like

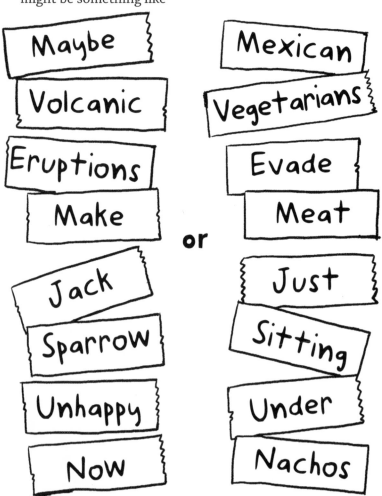

Maybe
Volcanic
Eruptions
Make

Jack
Sparrow
Unhappy
Now

or

Mexican
Vegetarians
Evade
Meat

Just
Sitting
Under
Nachos

Vote to find out what the silliest sentence is!

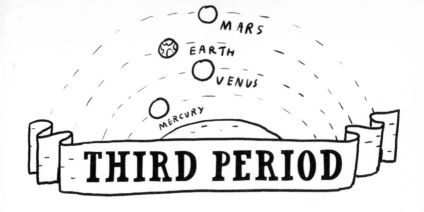

THIRD PERIOD

The Goldilocks Zone

You probably remember the story of Goldilocks, Junior Geniuses. She breaks into the house of the three bears and, because she is a terrible person, goes through all their stuff. At one point she tries three bowls of porridge that are cooling on the table. One is too hot. One is too cold. Luckily, the one in the middle is just right.

Inspired by this story, astronomers have invented the term "Goldilocks zone" to refer to the region around a star where habitable planets could possibly orbit. The Goldilocks zone is the ring around a star that isn't too hot for liquid surface water to exist, or too cold. It's just right.

TOO FAR   JUST RIGHT   TOO CLOSE

In our solar system the Goldilocks zone covers most of the rocky inner planets, which is where we're headed in this chapter. (Mercury is well within the "too hot" zone, but we'll pay it a brief visit too.) Now, that doesn't mean that Venus and Mars are hospitable to life. Mars doesn't have enough atmospheric pressure to sustain liquid water, as we'll see, while Venus has too much. But they're in the right neighborhood, anyway. Here on Earth, we got very, very lucky.

MERCURY

Picking On the Little Guy

Mercury is the smallest planet of the solar system, and also the innermost. Astronomers once believed there was another planet even closer to the Sun, called Vulcan. But Einstein's discovery of relativity in 1915 explained how Mercury's orbit actually works, and "Vulcan" was

relegated to the world of science fiction.

Given our current technology, it would take six years to travel to Mercury. And after all that anticipation, would it be worth it? Absolutely not.

Mercury is an atmosphere-less, crater-pelted wasteland—more or less like the Moon, but with even worse "weather." Because Mercury is more than twice as close to the Sun as Earth is, temperatures on the sunny side can get up to 800 degrees Fahrenheit, hot enough to melt tin and lead. On the dark side, meanwhile, Mercury is actually the *coldest* of the inner planets.

In 2013 the *MESSENGER* probe finished mapping the entire surface of Mercury, so we now know that, like the Moon, it has vast amounts of ice trapped at its poles. *MESSENGER* also

MESSENGER PROBE

explored the Caloris Basin, an impact crater big enough to hold the state of Texas! The explosion that formed the crater was so great that it created mile-high mountains and shock waves that traveled all the way through the planet.

Not a Bright Future

If Mercury sounds to you like it's no fun, don't worry—it may get the terrible fate it deserves. Some scientists predict that Jupiter's gravitational field will someday mess up Mercury's orbit so much that it will either crash into the Sun or fly out of the solar system entirely. Seven or eight billion years, Mercury. Just you wait.

Hot in Here

Can you imagine any place so terrible that it would actually make you miss Mercury? Well, class, welcome to Venus!

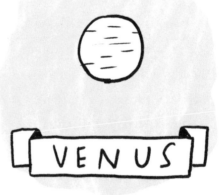

VENUS

Even though Venus receives about one-quarter the sunshine that Mercury does, the temperatures are much, much higher there—860 degrees Fahrenheit or so, even at night or at the poles. At those temperatures, you could

hold a large pizza in the air and it would be fully baked within one minute!

The terrible heat is a result of the greenhouse effect created by Venus's thick, cloudy atmosphere, which traps the Sun's heat instead of letting it escape into space.

Living the High Life

Some scientists have suggested that the only way to "beat the heat" on Venus would be to build colony cities that float thirty miles above the surface. At that elevation, temperature and pressure are Earth-like, and a bubble of breathable Earth atmosphere would float quite nicely in Venus's heavy carbon dioxide atmosphere. Picture the Cloud City of Bespin in *The Empire Strikes Back*—something like that!

Worst-Place Scenario

The heat is only the start of Venus's problems. The planet is almost the same size and mass as the Earth, but the similarities end there. A travel brochure to Venus might look something like this:

COME TO HELLISH VENUS!

OH BOY!

HURRICANE-FORCE WINDS, PLANETWIDE

MORE VOLCANOES THAN ANY OTHER PLANET!

Have you ever had one of those days that just seems to drag on forever? Maybe the last day of school before summer vacation? Well, Venus rotates so slowly that each day there really does go on and on—a single day there lasts almost eight Earth months. In fact, one Venusian day is longer than one Venusian year!

SULFURIC ACID RAIN!

VIOLENT LIGHTNING STORMS!

The pressure on Venus is so intense that just going for a stroll outside your rocket would be like walking three thousand feet below the surface of the Pacific. In fact, the atmosphere is so thick that some of the probes we've sent there didn't even need parachutes! They slowed down on their own before touching down.

DIM DAYS, PITCH BLACK NIGHTS!

MOUNTAINS TOPPED BY LEAD SNOW!

One Sweet Ride

The first human spacecraft ever to land on another planet were the Soviet Union's Venera probes, which were sent to Venus between 1961 and 1983. Most of these probes lasted only an hour or so in the harsh Venusian conditions, despite their sturdy engineering. *Venera 4* was even designed to work in case of a water landing—its antennae were closed with locks made of sugar, which would have melted when wet!

Venus is the only planet of the solar system named for a Roman goddess, not a god. So the nicest thing about the surface of Venus is that the craters have been named for famous women, from Cleopatra to Harriet Tubman to Laura Ingalls Wilder!

The Best and the Brightest

Venus is the kind of place that's best to enjoy from a distance—and luckily, it's easy to do just that, since it's the brightest object in the night sky except for the Moon. From Earth's point of view, Venus never gets far from the Sun, so it's only visible in our skies right before sunrise and right after sunset. The ancient Greeks and Egyptians actually believed Venus was two separate objects: a morning "star" and an evening one.

Venus is so big and bright that it can cast shadows at night, and is even visible during the daytime with the naked eye . . . if you know right where to look. With binoculars at night, you may even be able to see its sunlit side making a crescent shape, just like the Moon. Because of Venus's brightness and low position on the horizon, it's been mistaken for a UFO hundreds of times.

Cook Out

We do have Venus to thank for introducing us to a much nicer place, however: Australia! In 1769 King George III sent the explorer Captain Cook to the Southern Hemisphere to observe a "transit of Venus"—that's when Venus moves across the face of the Sun. On his way home Cook spotted an unknown coastline, becoming the first European to set foot on Australia! (By the way, I hope you caught the last transit of Venus on June 6, 2012, Junior Geniuses. There won't be another one until 2117!)

Earth

The Earth is pretty cool. There are forests and Wi-Fi here.

Red Planet

Earth's nearest planetary neighbor is Mars. It's still somewhere between 36 and 250 million miles away from us, depending on the orbits, but that's just a quick trip to the corner grocery store in cosmic terms.

Mars is also the planet where conditions are most like Earth. I don't mean that there are squirrels and McDonald's and football games every Sunday. But Mars does have:

- a twenty-four-hour day (more or less)
- a landscape that looks a lot like an Earth desert
- a surface area that's almost the same as Earth's dry land area (but no oceans, of course)
- temperatures that are only a little colder

There are big differences too. Mars is smaller, so gravity is just over a third what you're used to. You could do a long jump of ten feet or more. The sky there is red, but sunsets are blue—the exact opposite of Earth's sky. (The colors are due to Mars's dust storms, the worst in the solar system.) In the winter it gets cold enough for almost 25 percent of the atmosphere to freeze.

WEEEEEEE!

Doomed Moon

Unlike Earth, Mars has *two* moons: Deimos and Phobos, named for Greek gods of fear. They're tiny and not very round, and may be asteroids that were captured by Mars's gravity long, long ago. Phobos is falling toward Mars at the rate of six feet every year. Seven million years from now it will crash into a spiral of debris, and Mars will get its own ring, just like Saturn!

The Martian landscape is also more dramatic than any desert on Earth. There's Olympus Mons, a volcano the same size as Arizona. It's so big that there's nowhere on Mars, not even at the summit, where you can see the whole thing. There's a canyon called the Valles Marineris, which is four times deeper than the Grand Canyon and the length of the United States. The soil is a dull red color, due to iron oxides. That's right, Mars looks pinkish in the night sky thanks to good old ordinary rust.

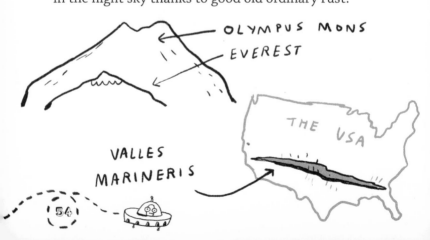

OLYMPUS MONS

EVEREST

VALLES MARINERIS

THE USA

Junior Genius Vocabulary Booster!

Remember, you can't call the soil on Mars "earth" because you're not on Earth. But it's not called "mars" either. The scientific term for dirt on other planets is "regolith," from the Greek for "rock blanket."

A Whole New World

Mars is an obvious first step off Earth for the human race, so we've sent dozens of missions to Mars. Two-thirds of them have failed. A 1998 Mars probe, *Climate Orbiter*, was destroyed for the dumbest of reasons: Engineers accidentally used pounds instead of the metric system when they were plotting its orbit! Next time a teacher tells you to be careful about the units in math problems, better pay attention!

But many probes have reached the Martian surface, and the latest ones carry robots designed to carefully explore it. The twin rovers *Spirit* and *Opportunity* both lasted over twenty-five times longer than their original mission plans, thanks in part to their efficient solar cells (and *Opportunity* is still going). Their successor, the *Curiosity* rover, is even better equipped.

MARS CURIOSITY ROVER

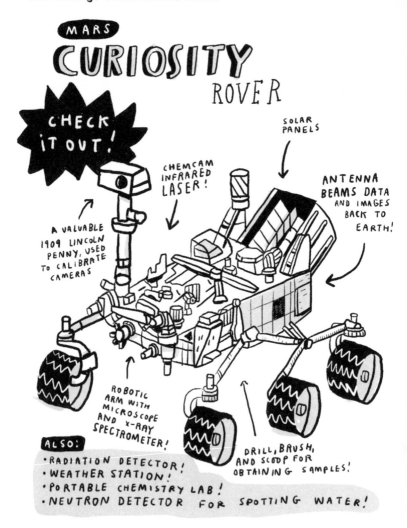

CHECK IT OUT!

SOLAR PANELS

CHEMCAM INFRARED LASER!

ANTENNA BEAMS DATA AND IMAGES BACK TO EARTH!

A VALUABLE 1909 LINCOLN PENNY, USED TO CALIBRATE CAMERAS

ROBOTIC ARM WITH MICROSCOPE AND X-RAY SPECTROMETER!

DRILL, BRUSH, AND SCOOP FOR OBTAINING SAMPLES!

ALSO:
- RADIATION DETECTOR!
- WEATHER STATION!
- PORTABLE CHEMISTRY LAB!
- NEUTRON DETECTOR FOR SPOTTING WATER!

These little guys are slow, traveling only a few inches a second at top speed, but they've now journeyed for miles and miles on Mars.

Elvis Lives!

NASA gives unofficial names to the rocks its rovers encounter, often inspired by the rocks' shapes. That's why Mars now has landmarks named . . .

VALENTINE

SCOOBY DOO

POT OF GOLD

TENNESSEE

POP TART

ELVIS

DARTH VADER

INDIANA JONES

Life on Mars

These rovers all have the same goal: to pave the way for *human* exploration of Mars. But that's going to be tough. There's almost no oxygen to breathe there, for one thing, so astronauts would need to wear pressure suits. And radiation levels are dangerously high.

Junior Genius Joviality

Q: Why did everyone hate the restaurant on Mars?

A: Because it had good food, but no atmosphere.

Since a mission to Mars would be much less expensive if the astronauts were not required to return to Earth, some scientists have predicted that the first humans on Mars will be permanent settlers. In 2013 a European space venture called Mars One, which is hoping to have its Martian base established by 2023, asked if anyone wanted to register for a one-way trip to the red planet. There were 202,586 volunteers!

Extra Credit

For a brief period in the 1960s, both the United States and the Soviet Union considered a Moon mission that would be a one-way trip! They'd shoot an astronaut (or cosmonaut, which is what Russian space travelers are called) at the Moon along with three years of supplies. "Okay, we'll pick you up as soon as we invent a way to do that!"

Living on Mars is a tough goal, but not an impossible one. For one thing, probes have revealed that Mars has much more water than we once thought. There are glaciers at the poles the size of Los Angeles and half a mile thick. Just one ice cap holds enough water to flood the entire Martian surface thirty-six feet deep. And tests show that the Martian soil has the right nutrients to grow crops like asparagus or green beans.

Someday that might be you, farming vegetables on the first human Mars colony. (I hope you like asparagus!)

Looking up at night, you'll see what looks like a bright double star. Nobody has ever seen it in the sky before. That's Earth and its moon, a hundred million miles away.

ART CLASS

"Three! Two! One! Liftoff!" The countdown that comes before a rocket launch is such a famous symbol of space exploration that the U.S. government actually changed the telephone area code of Florida's "Space Coast," where Cape Canaveral is located, from 407 to 321.

Space travel would never have been possible without Dr. Robert Goddard, who invented liquid-fuel rocketry. In 1920 he wrote an article speculating that human beings could one day travel to the Moon in rockets. The *New York Times* ran an editorial the next day, calling Goddard's theory that rockets would work in the vacuum of space "absurd." "[H]e only seems to lack the knowledge ladled out daily in high schools," sniffed the newspaper.

Goddard died in 1945, so he never lived to see rockets travel to the Moon. But on July 17, 1969, with Neil Armstrong and company en route to the Moon, the *Times* printed a correction. "[I]t is now definitely established that a rocket can function in a vacuum as well as in an atmosphere," they stated almost fifty years later. "The *Times* regrets the error."

You're probably too young to buy rocket fuel, Junior Geniuses, even on the Internet. But you can still design and launch your own rockets! All you need are:

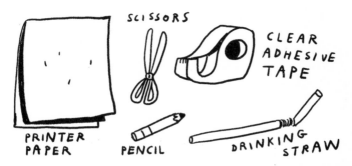

SCISSORS

CLEAR ADHESIVE TAPE

PRINTER PAPER

PENCIL

DRINKING STRAW

First, cut out a square of paper about five inches on a side. (If you want a brightly colored rocket, use scrapbooking paper rather than regular white paper. Construction paper is too heavy. Or color your printer paper yourself before you start building.) Wrap it tightly around a pencil and tape it together into a five-inch cylinder. Wiggle the pencil free.

Now your rocket needs a nose cone. Cut out a circle about two and a half inches in diameter and then remove a triangular wedge, like this. Pac-Man! Fold Pac-Man's two "lips" together to make a cone, and keep twirling it in on itself so the cone gets smaller. When it's as tight as you can get it, tape it together and then tape it to the top of your rocket tube. (If it's still too big, just trim down the bottom part of the cone until it's the same diameter as the cylinder.)

Now tape two fins to the rocket for stability. These are just paper triangles about two inches high and extending one inch from the rocket's base. Use a different color paper—*but only if you want your rocket to look awesome!*

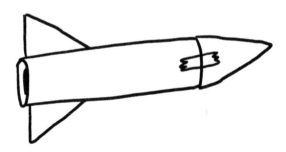

For Experts Only!

Prior to launch, decorate your rocket any way you like. I cannibalized some postage stamps to put flags on my rocket's fins, but that added a cost of forty-six cents per flag to my rocket, and NASA budgets are already pretty tight!

Place the rocket over a drinking straw. (The bendy kind will let you aim your rocket trajectory more easily.) Have a friend start a countdown, take a big lungful of air, and let her fly!

If you're unhappy with your launch, don't feel bad. Even Robert Goddard had some misfires. Experiment with different rocket sizes or fin shapes and see how far you can get your miniature mission to travel. If it gets stuck in a tree—well, I don't know what to tell you. That's a problem NASA's never had to deal with.

FOURTH PERIOD

Beyond the Asteroid Belt

We've now visited all the rocky planets in our solar system, Junior Geniuses. In this chapter we'll take a look at the other four planets, gas giants hundreds of times larger than the Earth. But to get there we'll have to dodge 2 million asteroids. Hey, if Han Solo can do it, we can do it.

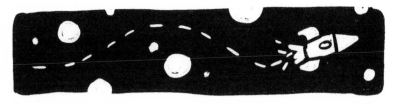

Rock Band

The solar system is full of lumpy chunks of rock much smaller than planets, called "planetoids" or "minor planets" or, most commonly, "asteroids."

Meteor Maker

Do you get confused by the differences among the various kinds of space rocks? Asteroids, meteors, meteorites? No need to feel ashamed! I'm here to help. Make a copy of this chart and carry it with you *at all times*.

ASTEROID — BIG LUMP OF ROCK HURTLING THROUGH SPACE

METEOROID — A TINY FRAGMENT OF AN ASTEROID

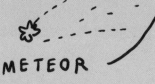

METEOR — THE "SHOOTING STAR" STREAK WHEN A METEOROID ENTERS EARTH'S ATMOSPHERE

METEORITE — SOLID DEBRIS THAT SURVIVES ITS CRASH TO EARTH

Many of these asteroids revolve around a region between the orbits of Mars and Jupiter. About half the mass of the asteroid belt is found in its four largest asteroids:

CERES   VESTA   PALLAS   HYGIEA

But there are almost 2 million others that are more than a kilometer wide.

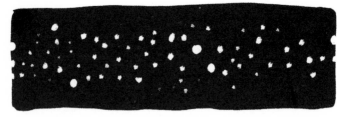

A few centuries ago astronomers thought that there had once been a fifth rocky planet between Mars and Jupiter, which they called Phaeton, and the asteroid belt was the rubble that was left when Phaeton got destroyed. Actually, the asteroid belt is debris that never got to *form* a planet, because Jupiter's gravity was always churning it around.

Asteroids are mostly made of carbon or silicate rock, but some are metallic, and they probably contain gold, platinum, and other valuable stuff. If we ever figure out how to send miners to the minor planets, NASA estimates that the minerals there would be worth $100 billion—for every single person on Earth!

Space Mountain

In 2011 probes revealed that 90 percent of Vesta is covered by a single impact crater, called Rheasilvia. The peak at the center of Rheasilvia is almost as high as Olympus Mons on Mars, which at 16 miles high is probably the biggest mountain in our solar system!

Catch a Falling Star

Odds are you'll never go gold mining in the asteroid belt and earn your $100 billion. But little bits of asteroids are all around us, in the form of meteorites (see page 65). Here are the five most important things to know about meteorites.

There are a lot of them. Almost 300 meteors fly through our atmosphere *every second*. Earth gains 90 tons of mass every day from all this new space stuff.

They're cold! Even though meteors heat up and glow when they first enter the Earth's atmosphere, they cool down as they fall. Most land with frost on them.

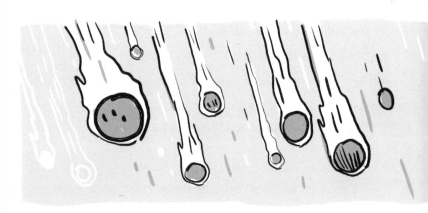

They come in showers. On April 26, 1803, thousands of meteorite fragments rained down on the tiny town of L'Aigle, France. They made such a racket that they even woke up sleeping villagers!

They get pretty big. The heaviest meteorite ever discovered is the Hoba West—but if you want to see it, you'll have to fly to the African country of Namibia. It's 66 tons of solid iron, so it's staying put.

Duck! In 1908 a meteor (or possibly a comet) exploded over Tunguska, Siberia, knocking over 80 million trees. There are no verified accounts of meteorites ever killing anyone, but every so often someone gets bonked on the head. In 1954 a woman named Ann Hodges was sitting in her living room in Sylacauga, Alabama, when a grapefruit-size meteorite fell through her roof, bounced off the radio, and smashed into her, giving her quite the bruise.

Homework

The annual Perseid and Leonid meteor showers can put on quite a show. Mark the weeks of August 12 and November 17 on your calendar and, on a clear night, go outside and look up. Be patient. Every few minutes, you might see a new "falling star."

Big Daddy

Can you imagine how big Jupiter must be, Junior Geniuses? It's bigger than all the other planets, asteroids, and comets in the solar system put together. Take a moment to picture Jupiter. *Wrong! It's even bigger than that.*

Jupiter is so big that it has a moon that's larger than a planet.

Jupiter is so big that most early cultures named it after their chief god. In Greece it was "Zeus," in India it was "Brihaspati," and in Egypt it was "Amon."

Jupiter is so big that when we send probes to the outer planets, we often use Jupiter's immense gravity to accelerate them.

Jupiter is so big that it has a storm on its surface as large as three Earths! It's called the Great Red Spot, and it's been brewing for centuries. We've seen lightning in the Great Red Spot that's thousands of times brighter than the puny bolts here on Earth.

Extra Credit

Even though Jupiter is the largest planet, it has the shortest day in the solar system, just under ten hours. Jupiter spins so fast that its equator bulges out into space six thousand extra miles!

Unlike the inner, rocky planets, the gas giants of the outer solar system don't really have a surface. If you were falling toward Jupiter, its swirling atmosphere (mostly hydrogen and helium) would just get thicker and denser as you fell. Eventually the atmosphere gets so dense that it becomes a liquid ocean of metallic hydrogen 25,000 miles deep. There's probably a small iron core down there somewhere, but you'll be squished long before you hit it.

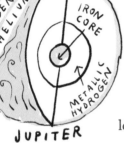

JUPITER

Bonus Junior Genius Vocabulary Booster!

Martians are from Mars, but what kind of aliens would come from Jupiter? Jupiterians? The adjective for Jupiter is actually "Jovian."

Many Moons Ago

Even though it's a really big ball of hydrogen and helium, Jupiter never gobbled up enough mass while the solar system was forming to become a star. But it's still the center of its own miniature solar system of a kind: So far, astronomers have spotted sixty-seven moons orbiting Jupiter!

Don't worry, Junior Geniuses. I'm not going to make you memorize them for the test. Most of the Jovian moons are tiny little things, so small that if you took a running leap off the surface, you'd float right into space. Many of them are so unimportant to astronomers that they don't have real names, just codes like "S/2003 J 18."

The four large moons, however, are pretty interesting. They're called the "Galilean moons," after the

astronomer Galileo, who spotted them through a telescope in 1610. They were the first new objects discovered in the solar system since prehistoric times.

IO. The tidal forces of Jupiter and the other moons make this the most geologically active place in the solar system. Some lava fountains on Io spew lava up to 250 miles into space from an underground ocean of magma that's hotter than all of Earth's volcanoes put together! Away from the volcanoes, the rest of the moon is covered in snow.

EUROPA. Actually has more water than Earth! Europa is probably the likeliest place we might find alien life in our solar system. We've discovered colonies of sea creatures living in the sunless depths of Earth's oceans near warm hydrothermal vents. Could there be similar ecosystems on Europa?

GANYMEDE. This is the largest moon in the solar system—it's even bigger than Mercury! It has a liquid saltwater ocean underneath layers of rock and ice.

CALLISTO. The white spots are craters—probably made by asteroids smashing through surface rock to reveal ice beneath. Callisto has more craters than any other member of the solar system.

Ringside Seats

All four of the gas giants have systems of dusty rings circling them, but Saturn is something else. Its rings are the most remarkable in the solar system. Well, except for onion rings. Let's be honest, onion rings are pretty good.

CLOSE UP

Saturn's rings look like a solid hoop or series of bands. But they're not. Take a closer look: They're actually countless particles of ice, ranging in size from grains of sand to mountains. They're probably debris from a moon that was destroyed billions of years ago.

Because they're made of water ice, Saturn's rings are bright and shiny, so prominent that you can see them in the night sky with a good pair of binoculars. (The other planets will look like round dots, but Saturn will be oval.) But every decade or so the rings disappear completely from Earth's viewpoint. This will happen next in March 2025. You see, Saturn's rings are incredibly thin for their size: 125,000 miles long, but much less than a mile thick. Proportionally, that's like a sheet of tissue paper the size of a football field! So when you look at them edge on . . . they vanish!

Extra Credit

In 2009 a new, very faint ring of Saturn was discovered, millions of miles outside the other rings. The Phoebe ring is so big that, if we could see it from Earth, it would be twice the size of the full Moon!

Saturn is the least dense planet in the solar system—just 0.69 grams per cubic centimeter. This makes it less dense than water, meaning that Saturn would actually float in water, if you could find an ocean big enough to dip it in!

Pop Quiz!

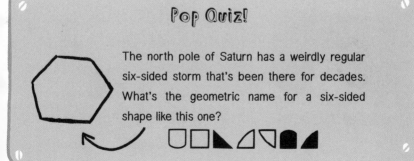

The north pole of Saturn has a weirdly regular six-sided storm that's been there for decades. What's the geometric name for a six-sided shape like this one?

Saturnian Satellites

Like its big brother Jupiter, Saturn has sixty-something moons, most of which are tiny. The ones to know are:

PANDORA. Not the one from *Avatar*. This Pandora is small and football-shaped.

JANUS and **EPIMETHEUS.** Only thirty miles apart, but they never collide. Instead, they switch places every few years.

MIMAS. Thanks to a big crater, called Herschel, it looks like the Death Star! But it is not, as far as we know, a giant Imperial space station.

ENCELADUS. Has giant "cryovolcanoes" that shoot out ice and snow instead of lava!

RHEA. May have its own ring system, which would make it the only known ringed moon in the solar system.

TITAN. An Earth-like place with oceans, rivers, and lakes—but filled with liquid methane, not water. European scientists are planning to send a floating probe called *TALISE* to Titan to study it—which would be the first boat in space! The skies on Titan are orange, and the mountains are all named for mountains from J. R. R. Tolkien's Middle-earth.

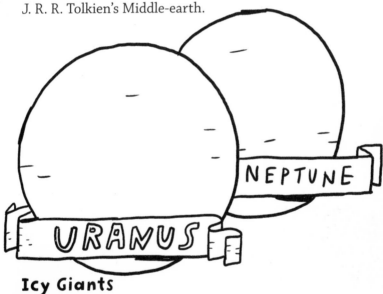

Icy Giants

Unlike Jupiter and Saturn, the other two gas giants, Uranus and Neptune, have thick layers of ice deep inside them. But this isn't like the normal Earth ice you'd see in a cooler or a punch bowl. It's actually really, really hot! The only thing keeping it "frozen" into a solid is the high pressures deep within these planets.

Like most parts of space, the ice giants are also really, really terrible places to be. Neptune has jet-stream winds whirling around it at twice the speed of sound. You'd be ripped in half immediately if you tried to visit.

But if you do make the trip, be sure to fill your pockets. The high pressure in the atmospheres of Uranus and Neptune can squeeze methane gas so hard that it crystallizes. It literally rains diamonds there!

Curious George

Uranus's discoverer, William Herschel, originally named it for England's King George III. That's right, Junior Geniuses: We almost had a planet named George! Luckily, more sensible heads prevailed and decided to give the new planet a much more dignified, less silly name, one that nobody could ever possibly make jokes about: Uranus.

One of These Things Is Not Like the Other

Most of the stuff in the solar system orbits the Sun in nearly the same plane, which we call the *ecliptic* ("eh-KLIP-tick"). And most of them rotate on an axis more or less perpendicular to the ecliptic. Which one doesn't belong?

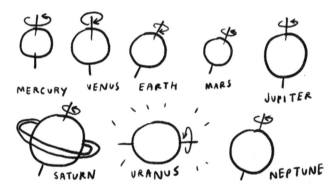

Yup, Uranus does its own thing—it's the only planet in the solar system that rotates "on its side." No one is sure why.

Left Out in the Cold

Of course, there used to be one more planet in the solar system, sometimes as far as a billion miles beyond Neptune. And then, a few years ago, it officially lost its job. Between its discovery in 1930 and its demotion in

2006, it hadn't even gotten the chance to go around the Sun *once*! What happened to poor Pluto?

What happened is that space telescopes began to find many more Pluto-like objects out at the fringes of the solar system. We gave them strange names like Quaoar, Makemake, Haumea, and Sedna. One of these "trans-Neptunian objects," as scientists called them, was Eris—which was even bigger than Pluto. So what do we do? Make *all* of them planets?

Well, scientists decided that they *were* all planets . . . sort of. Now they're called "dwarf planets." Pluto and all its friends got kicked out of the club of *real* planets.

Land of the Freeze

Pluto is so far away that the Sun is just a dot in its sky, about as bright as a full moon but much smaller. But you'd freeze solid before you got a chance to enjoy the view much. The Plutonian surface is ice frozen harder than steel and dusted with a pinkish-brown snow of frozen carbon dioxide, nitrogen, and methane.

Pluto was discovered by a scientist named Clyde Tombaugh, who loved astronomy but never got to go to college because his parents were poor farmers. As a young man he built his own telescopes and sketched pictures of the surfaces of Jupiter and Mars. When he sent them off to an observatory, they were so impressed that they offered him a job!

Tombaugh died in 1997, but some of his ashes are currently in the *New Horizons* space probe, on its way to Pluto right now. So there you go, Junior Geniuses. Even when the odds are against you, if you have a dream in life, you can go far. But right now, my dream is to get you out of this classroom. Because it's time for lunch.

LUNCH

A quick lunch on Earth is easy. Make a sandwich, grab an apple, pour yourself a glass of milk. But in space the same meal would be a huge hassle. In zero gravity little bubbles of milk would get everywhere. The apples would have to be treated with a chlorine solution to sanitize them for their journey. Space sandwiches come in little cubes, which can be eaten in one bite without crumbs flying away.

MMM... BACON.

You see, space food is designed to feed astronauts as well as possible while taking up as little space as possible. For example, instead of bacon, the Apollo astronauts ate "bacon squares" that had been squished with a hydraulic press! There are other considerations too. NASA had a longtime ban on foods

like beans and broccoli that can lead to, um, unpleasant sounds and smells in a small space capsule.

Since the beginning of space travel, astronauts have taken along snacks in case they got hungry. Yuri Gagarin, the first Russian in space, brought a tube of soup. John Glenn ate applesauce. But most of the food was pretty unappetizing. Aboard

Gemini 3, the astro-

naut John Young broke NASA rules by smuggling along a corned beef sandwich from his favorite New York–style deli and offering it to his crewmate, Gus Grissom. The scandal over the contraband sandwich even reached Congress, and Young received a formal reprimand from NASA.

I still wouldn't go to space just for the food, but things are much better today. Astronauts aboard the International Space Station get their choice of more than three hundred meals, including the occasional fresh fruit and vegetables, and can even request favorite snacks from home. One Canadian astronaut got tubes of maple syrup. South Korea spent millions of dollars on a space-friendly form of its national pickled-cabbage dish, kimchi, for its astronauts. So much for no unpleasant smells in a small space capsule!

When they weren't smuggling sandwiches, the astronauts of the 1960s and '70s brought 842 pounds of geological samples home from the Moon. Here's a recipe for an edible version of those moon rocks that you can enjoy right here on Earth.

Moon Rocks

- 1 CUP CORN SYRUP
- 1 CUP SUGAR
- 1 TEASPOON VANILLA
- 1 CUP PEANUT BUTTER (CREAMY)
- 6 CUPS CORNFLAKES

- 2 BAGS CANDY MELTS, ONE WHITE AND ONE BLACK (YOU CAN FIND THESE AT CRAFT STORES OR ONLINE)
- 1/3 CUP CANOLA OIL
- WAXED PAPER

Directions

1. Mix the corn syrup and sugar over medium heat, stirring constantly. Make sure you get help from Mission Control (a grown-up) before using the stove.

2. Bring the mixture to a boil for one minute, then remove from heat.

3. Blend in the vanilla and peanut butter, followed by the cornflakes.

4. When the mixture is cool enough to touch but not yet fully set, shape it into "rocks" and place them on waxed paper. These could be round balls or any shape you like. (For this part you will definitely want a grown-up's help. The Moon hasn't been volcanically active for 3 billion years, but these lunar lumps can burn you if you're not careful. It might help for the person forming the "rocks" to dip their hands in cold water.)

5. Melt the black and white candy melts separately. A pair of glass bowls in the microwave works well. Alternate short bursts of power with stirring until the candy is fully melted.

6. Mix the black and white candy coatings together to get the gray color of your choice. (More white than black makes for a good Moon color.) Add the canola oil one tablespoon at a time until the coating has a runny consistency.

7. Dip the rocks in the bowl of candy coating and replace them on the waxed paper. You're done! Wait for your specimens to cool and share them with some fellow space travelers. That's seven small steps for a man, one great snack for mankind.

FIFTH PERIOD

Lost in the Stars

Our Sun, of course, is a star. It's a very important star to us, since it grows our food and warms our beaches and inspires Beatles songs. But it's far from the only star.

Go outside at night and look up. A lot of stars, right? Not really. There are only three thousand stars or so visible in the night sky at any given time. If you counted one a second, you'd be done in . . . about forty-five minutes.

But here's the thing. For every star you can see, there are lots that you can't. "Billions and billions!" as the famed astronomer Carl Sagan used to say.

There are:

5,000–8,000 stars visible to the naked eye from Earth

15,000,000 stars visible with a small telescope

400,000,000,000,000 stars in the Milky Way galaxy

1,000,000,000,000,000,000,000,000 stars in the observable universe

In other words, about a hundred thousand stars for every grain of sand on every beach or desert on Earth.

That's a lot of stars.

ONE...
TWO...

Welcome to the Main Sequence!

Like people, stars come in many different colors and sizes. But, deep down, people are pretty much the same no matter how they look on the outside. Not so with stars.

Scientists usually classify stars on a graph like this, which is called a Hertzsprung-Russell diagram.

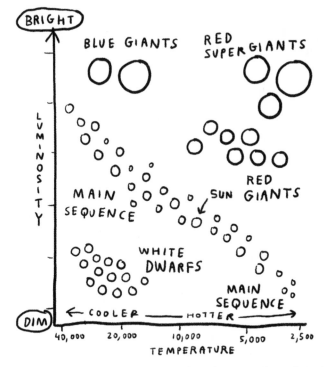

Each star gets plotted on this diagram based on its *spectral class* (a letter code that corresponds to its surface temperature) and its *luminosity* (the amount of energy it radiates). For example, our Sun is the temperature of a G-type star with a luminosity of 1, so it gets plotted along the "main sequence," along with most other stars in the universe—about 90 percent of them.

But not all of them! If a star is much bigger or smaller than our Sun, it can act very differently.

Official Junior Genius Way to Remember Spectral Classes

There are seven different letters for the temperature classes of stars. From hot to cool, they are O, B, A, F, G, K, and M. The common way to remember this list is with this sentence:

"O, be a fine girl (or guy), kiss me!"

But I don't want any mushy talk like that in my classroom! You are all too young to be kissing fine girls and guys. But I know you do work hard in school, so instead, just remember this sentence:

"Oh boy, an 'F' grade kills me!"

You're the Star!

The life cycle of a star lasts billions of years. To understand it better, we're going to speed things up a little.

1

You are a protostar, formed by the collapse of a giant molecular cloud called a stellar nursery, where stars are born!

• •

If you have enough mass to become a star, turn to section 3.

• •

If you are too little, turn to section 6.

2

You use up your hydrogen very slowly, but even if it takes a trillion years, it starts to run low sometime. You burn through the last 10 percent of it very quickly, heating into a blue dwarf before running out altogether.

• •

Turn to section 7.

Your hydrogen ignites and fusion begins! Soon you are on the main sequence of the Hertzsprung-Russell diagram.

. . . .

If you are smaller than Earth's Sun, turn to section 4.

. . . .

If you are about the size of Earth's Sun, turn to section 5.

. . . .

If you are much more massive than Earth's Sun, turn to section 9.

4

You are a red dwarf, the most common type of star in our galaxy. You are small and cool.

. . . .

If you are less than one-quarter the Sun's mass, turn to section 2.

. . . .

If you are bigger than that, turn to section 14.

5

You are a yellow dwarf star. For about 10 billion years, you "glow" about your business. If you have a planetary system, life may evolve on it. Good job!

· ·

Turn to section 14.

6

You are a brown dwarf, somewhere between fifteen and seventy-five times the mass of Jupiter. That's just not big enough for hydrogen fusion to begin. Astronomers call you a "failed star," which hurts a little deep down.

· ·

The End.

7

You are a very dense white dwarf—about the mass of the Sun, but squeezed into a ball the size of the Earth. You are hot at first, but cool off very quickly.

· ·

Turn to section 15.

8

Fine, you have expanded into a red supergiant, but you can't help feeling that something explosive is still going to happen.

If you are ready for that now, turn to section 13.

If you'd like to be a supergiant a little longer, turn to section 9.

9

You have become a blue supergiant, blindingly bright and hot. Your core is going to collapse one of these eons, you know.

If you are ready for that, turn to section 13.

If you'd like to be a supergiant a little longer, turn to section 8.

10

You collapse into a black hole, just a few miles wide but unbelievably dense. Your gravity is so great that not even light—or this story—can escape.

• •

The End.

11

You eject your outer layers of gas, like a butterfly emerging from its chrysalis. These brightly colored clouds of gas become a planetary nebula, leaving only your core behind.

• •

Turn to section 7.

12

You collapse into a neutron star. A single spoonful of you weighs as much as a mountain. You gradually cool and fade to black.

• •

The End.

BOOM! You are a supernova, sending almost all your mass out into space at a speed of 18,000 miles per second. The resulting shock wave will expand for two centuries.

If you were a colossally, mind-boggling big star before, turn to section 10.

If you were merely amazingly big, turn to section 12.

14

You are out of hydrogen. You gradually cool and grow into a red giant. If you have planets, you eventually engulf them as you expand.

Turn to section 11.

15

You are now a black dwarf and no longer emit any heat or light. Trillions of years have passed. What did it all mean?

The End.

STAR

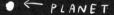 ← PLANET

Night Watch

If you'd rather enjoy the stars from a distance, Junior Geniuses, I recommend going outside and trying some stargazing of your own. A few basic tips to remember:

Light is the enemy! The darker the night, the better the view will be. Avoid city lights as much as you can. If you're planning to check out stars and not the Moon, wait for a night when the Moon won't be up.

It's dark out there. Don't bump into things! Even more importantly, give your eyes twenty to thirty minutes to adjust to the dark. They'll become ten thousand times more sensitive during that half hour, because the human body is an amazing thing.

Stars are not planets. Because planets look larger in the sky than stars do, the Earth's atmosphere doesn't distort their light as much. If the little dot you're looking at "twinkles," it's a star. If it's fairly steady, it's a planet

(Mercury, Venus, Mars, Jupiter, or Saturn). If it's red and blinks, it's an airplane.

Try binoculars. As we learned, only three thousand stars are visible to the naked eye at any given time, even on the clearest night. But a good pair of binoculars bumps that number *a lot*—by a few hundred thousand, even.

Out of Focus

In the 1980s astronomers found a way to stargaze without that pesky atmosphere getting in the way: They put a telescope in orbit around the Earth. The Hubble Space Telescope was designed to be so powerful that it could see the glowing butt of a single firefly 10,000 miles away!

Unfortunately, NASA discovered that their new toy was taking blurry photographs because one of its mirrors was a *tiny* bit too shallow—like, by about one-fiftieth the width of a human hair. (The problem was later tracked down to a single speck of paint that messed up the mirror-polishing tests!) Even more unfortunately, they didn't discover this until Hubble was already in space. But a multibillion-dollar space shuttle repair mission got Hubble back on its feet, and it's been making amazing space discoveries ever since.

Star Search

So which stars should you be looking for? The sky's the limit, of course, but here are some ideas to start with.

The Brightest Star. Sirius is named for the Greek word for "glowing," and boy, does it ever. It's twice as bright as any other star in the night sky. Sirius is found in the constellation Canis Major (the "greater dog"), so it's nicknamed the Dog Star. The ancient Romans noticed that Sirius rose just before dawn during July and August, which is why we still call the hottest part of the summer the "dog days."

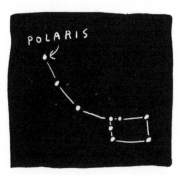

The Pole Star. See the two stars that form the edge of the Big Dipper's cup? Follow that same path upward, and the first bright star you reach will be Polaris, the handle of the Little Dipper. Explorers have long used Polaris to navigate by. It's called the "North Star," because it's the closest bright star to the celestial north pole, the point in the sky that all the other constellations seem to spin around. (Actually, it's the Earth that's spinning, of course.)

Extra Credit!

The Earth's rotation actually wobbles on its axis a bit, so the pole star changes over time. About five thousand years ago, a star called Thuban was due north. In the year 10,000 the blue supergiant Deneb will be the pole star.

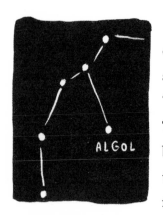

The Demon Star. Arab astronomers named the second brightest star in the constellation Perseus "Algol," meaning "the ghoul." They thought Algol was creepy because it "winks"—every 68 and three-quarters hours, its light dims for a few hours. Today we know Algol's secret: It's actually a binary star system, with two suns whirling around each other. When the dimmer star passes in front of the brighter one, Algol winks.

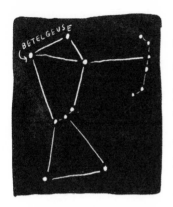

The Enormous Star. In the armpit of the constellation of Orion glows Betelgeuse—and yes, astronomers pronounce it "beetle juice," so you can too. On a dark night, Betelgeuse will look distinctly more orange than its neighbors. It's a red supergiant, which means that it's *huge*, one thousand times larger than the Sun. If it *were* our Sun, we'd all be on fire right now, because its surface would extend almost all the way out to the orbit of Jupiter!

The Dying Star. The stars are light-years away from Earth, so the images we see of them took decades, centuries, or even millennia to get here. Deneb, for example, is believed to be 2,600 light-years away, which means we're just now seeing light that it radiated around the time the Roman Republic was founded. Looking into the stars is like a time machine, Junior Geniuses. We are only seeing their ghosts.

In some cases this might be literal—we might be seeing stars that are already dead! One good candidate is Eta Carinae, which has been flickering wildly for centuries. Astronomers believe it's at the end of its lifespan, and could explode as a supernova anytime. Who knows? Maybe it'll go tonight. Keep watching the skies.

Extra Credit

Earth's closest star neighbor after the Sun, on the other hand, is the Alpha Centauri star system, located just 4.37 light-years away from us. It's close by and very bright—and yet the ancient Greek and Arab astronomers never studied it, and you can't either. Why? Because Alpha Centauri is visible, for the most part, only from the Southern Hemisphere!

Boom Boom Pow!

If Eta Carinae does go supernova, it'll be something to see. Supernovas only last for a few days, but they can burn as bright as an entire galaxy.

The brightest star explosion ever recorded on Earth happened in the constellation Lupus in the year 1006. We have records of the "new star" being spotted all over the globe, in Europe, Egypt, Iraq, China, and Japan. A Chinese historian said the explosion was half the size of the Moon! That would make it bright enough to read by at night!

Supernovas are the most likely place in the universe for elements heavier than oxygen to form. The sodium in your saltshaker, the gold in your jewelry, even the iron and calcium in your body were all probably born in an ancient supernova. Those elements spread through space billions of years ago, and some became part of our newly forming solar system. In other words, you have star stuff inside you!

Pop Quiz!

Speaking of heavy things in stars, Junior Geniuses: In 2004 British scientists discovered a white dwarf known as BPM 37093, which they nicknamed "Lucy." The entire core of this star is a single 2,500-mile-wide ball of crystallized carbon. In other words, this star is the galaxy's largest what?

Lord of the Dense

When supernovas collapse, they *really* collapse. In fact, their atoms squish so tightly together that the neutrons in them actually touch each other. This takes the whole mass of a star and compresses it into a ball just ten miles

wide. Picture a star bigger than our Sun squeezed down so it fits into Washington, DC, and you can start to imagine what neutron stars are like. Just a teaspoon from one would weigh as much as 900 Great Pyramids of Giza.

This incredible density makes neutron stars act pretty weird. Unlike most stars, they probably have a solid, very smooth surface—like steel, only 10 billion times stronger. And they're fast, too. A neutron star can spin up to 43,000 times per minute on its axis without getting ripped apart.

Even light would be bent around it by its intense gravity, so if you stood next to a neutron star, you could see around to what was on the back of it! But I don't

recommend getting that close. You'd be sucked in so hard that every nucleus of every atom in your body would be smashed apart on the neutron's surface.

Radio Stars

Some neutron stars become *pulsars*, sending a beam of radio waves out into space as they spin. From Earth this looks like a flashing pulse, as if from some kind of cosmic lighthouse. The timing can be as precise as any atomic clock ever invented. The first pulsar ever discovered hasn't varied by a hundred-millionth of a second in the decades since it was found.

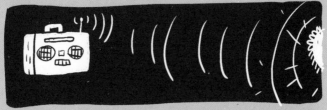

Others become *magnetars*, with incredibly strong magnetic fields that spit X-rays and gamma rays into space. Their magnetic pull is so intense that they could erase the strip on a credit card sitting in a wallet 100,000 miles away!

MUSIC CLASS

Ancient philosophers once believed that the Sun, the Moon, and other astronomical bodies moved with a form of harmony that was almost musical—they called this the "music of the spheres." The English composer Gustav Holst even wrote a suite called *The Planets*, in which each of the planets got its own theme song. (The suite had only seven movements, because I guess Earth doesn't count and Pluto hadn't been discovered yet. In 2000 a composer named Colin Matthews added a new movement for Pluto—only to have his work go to waste six years later when astronomers decide to take away Pluto's planetary status.)

Today we know that planets don't literally play music (except maybe for Freddie Mercury and Bruno Mars). Sound can't be heard in a vacuum, for one thing, so outer space is a very quiet place. Any space movie you've ever seen where spaceships go **WHOOOOSH!** or explosions go **BOOOOM!** is a big lie.

In 2003, however, astronomers discovered that a gigantic black hole in the center of the faraway Perseus A cluster was putting out sound waves. In fact, the black hole was rumbling away at a pitch a million billion times lower than your ear can hear! Scientists called it the "lowest note known in the universe." Specifically, the black hole is humming a B flat . . . fifty-seven octaves lower than middle C. To play that note, a piano keyboard would have to be about thirty feet long!

When humans go into space, they often break the silence with their own songs. The first space song ever was broadcast on December 16, 1965, after the astronauts aboard *Gemini 6* smuggled sleigh bells and a harmonica into their capsule. In a holiday mood, they reported to Mission Control that they had seen a strange satellite in a polar orbit: a command module piloted by someone in a red suit and being pulled by eight smaller modules. In other words, Santa Claus! Then they began to play "Jingle Bells" on their instruments.

Ever since the Apollo missions, astronauts in space have received a daily musical "wake-up call" from Houston, ranging from rock to jazz to country to classical. In 2005 Paul McCartney played the Beatles hit "Good Day Sunshine" live for the crew of the space shuttle *Atlantis*.

Sometimes the astronauts reply with music of their own. In 2013 the Canadian astronaut Chris Hadfield played a zero-gravity cover version of David Bowie's song "Space Oddity," which became a YouTube sensation. And the *Curiosity* rover beamed the will.i.am song "Reach for the Stars" back to Earth in 2012, making him the first rapper to have an interplanetary hit!

SIXTH PERIOD

Expanding Universe

Mark my words, Junior Geniuses. Someday, perhaps when you are a very old person, being spoon-fed space-soup by a robot, August 25, 2012, may be remembered as one of the most important dates in  human history. Neil Armstrong, the first man on the Moon, died that day. But that's not the most important space thing that happened.

The big news that day came from the Kuiper Belt, on the outskirts of our solar system. On that date, the *Voyager 1* spacecraft crossed the *heliopause*, the border where the Sun's solar wind stops "blowing." To scientists that's the official line where interstellar space begins. On August 25, 2012, for the first time, a human probe left the solar system.

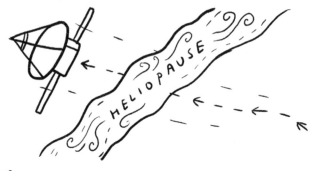

The Long Haul

Here's how big the solar system is, Junior Geniuses. NASA launched *Voyager 1* way back in 1977, when your parents probably dressed like this:

Even traveling at 38,000 miles per hour, its current speed, it took *Voyager* thirty-five years to enter interstellar space.

And here's how big space is. It'll take *Voyager* another forty thousand years to reach the neighborhood of its first star! (Unfortunately, its batteries are scheduled to run down around the year 2025, so if it finds anything interesting out there, it won't be able to tell us about it.)

Let's follow *Voyager* out of our solar system to see what else it might pass as it ventures into a vast, expanding universe.

Extra Credit

Beyond the Kuiper Belt, where Pluto and its little dwarf friends play, *Voyager* will also have to pass through the Oort cloud, a huge sphere of little icy chunks that occasionally come our way as comets. Some astronomers even think that there's a ninth planet—a gas giant called Tyche ("TIE-kee")—out in the Oort cloud, whose gravity hurls these comets at Earth.

Nothing's Gonna Stop Me Now

In addition to being big, space is very, very empty. Of course it is. That's why we call it "space." If it were full of stuff everywhere, we would probably call it "outer stuff." Imagine a building twenty miles long, twenty miles wide, and twenty miles high that contains nothing but a single grain of sand. That's roughly the emptiness of space.

Star Burst

Here's the first question everyone has about the vacuum of space: Could I survive in it? The answer is "Yes . . . but not very long." NASA experiments suggest that you would *not* explode if you suddenly found yourself floating naked in deep space. You might get cold, or sunburned, or have some ear trouble, but thirty seconds of space exposure wouldn't have any permanent effects at all, and it would take a minute or two to become fatal. Here's a helpful tip if an evil computer ever pushes you out of an airlock or something: exhale. Holding your breath seems smart, but all that internal pressure will mess up your organs.

But for the last fifty years or so, scientists have been discovering that ordinary matter—the kind of stuff that you and I and chairs and ducks and sandwiches and planets are made of—makes up only about 4 percent of the mass of the universe. What's the other 96 percent? *We don't really know.*

It seems that 23 percent of the universe is made up of a mysterious, completely invisible substance we call "dark matter."

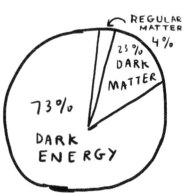

REGULAR
MATTER
4%

23%
DARK
MATTER

73%
DARK
ENERGY

We can tell that it's out there exerting gravity—enough gravity to hold galaxies together, even. But we have no idea what it is, because, at least for now, it's completely undetectable.

And 73 percent of the universe is something even weirder: a gravity-defying force we call "dark energy," because that sounds better than "what the heck is this crazy stuff?!?" It's one of the great mysteries of science today.

The part of the universe that we *can* see emits light. Astronomers once thought that the average color of the universe was a pale bluish white that they called "**cosmic turquoise**." But in 2002 they realized they had made a mistake in their math, and the *actual* color of the universe is a creamy, pale-brown shade. The scientists voted on names for the new color.

Astronomer Almond?

Big Bang Beige?

Primordial Clam Chowder?

In the end, the winning name was "**cosmic latte**," named for a milky coffee drink. (The guy who suggested it happened to read about the new research while sipping a latte at Starbucks.) So if you're ever drawing a picture of the universe, Junior Geniuses, you know which crayon to use.

Scent into Orbit

Space may be empty, but that doesn't mean it doesn't smell! Astronauts returning from space walks often report that the void has a very distinct odor: a mix of hot metal, exhaust fumes, and seared steak! This is the result of smelly molecules called hydrocarbons, emitted from dying stars.

Farther out in space, the chemistry gets different. If *Voyager* had a nose, it might find itself passing through zones that smelled sweet and others that stank like rotten eggs. Recently, scientists studying a dust cloud at the center of the Milky Way found traces of ethyl formate, a chemical that gives raspberries their flavor. In other words, the heart of our galaxy smells like raspberries!

The Hole Truth

In our last chapter, we saw that stars can sometimes collapse into incredibly heavy objects called black holes. A black hole is the darkest black you can imagine, because its gravity is so strong that not even light can escape.

Scientists have been speculating about super-dense "dark stars" since 1783, but black holes were just a theory until few decades ago, when bursts of X-rays were spotted coming from a mysterious object called Cygnus X-1. Many astronomers thought these rays could be a result of matter getting sucked into a black hole. The famous physicist Stephen Hawking doubted that

STEPHEN HAWKING

Cygnus was a black hole, and even made a wager with his colleague Kip Thorne that it wasn't. But by 1990 there was just too much evidence that this was, indeed, the first black hole ever discovered, and Hawking paid up.

Not all black holes are the corpses of dead stars. It's believed all big galaxies, including our own, have supermassive black holes at their centers, billions of times as large as the Sun. In fact, one of our nearest galactic neighbors, M106*, has two weird "anomalous arms" that don't seem to follow the galaxy's typical spiral shape. Astronomers now think that these arms are the result of M106's black hole shooting out blasts of lethal cosmic radiation thousands of light-years long! The center of that galaxy is a massive death ray millions of times more powerful than our own Sun.

* Galaxies and nebulae bright enough to be visible to earth are given "M" numbers named for Charles Messier, the French astronomer who first catalogued them.

118

Pop Quiz!

Scientists studying ancient cedar tree rings in Japan think that a mysterious spike in radiation in the year 774 may be a result of two black holes colliding! This massive collision would have caused a burst of what dangerous rays, named for the Greek letter that comes after alpha and beta?

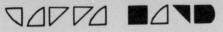

Pasta, Present, and Future

What if *Voyager* were to get sucked into a black hole as it makes its way through our galaxy? What if *you* somehow traveled into one? What would it be like?

Well, I can't say I recommend it. Black holes are so dense, said Einstein, that they can even *distort time*. So as you approach the edge of the black hole, the "point of no return" that scientists call the *event horizon*, time begins to slow down for you. A faraway observer would see you gradually slow down and stop just at the edge of the black hole. If you could somehow back up from the edge after staying there awhile, you'd find that you had time-traveled thousands of years into the future!

This "time dilation" effect means that you can look ahead of you and see everything that has ever fallen into the black hole in the past. Behind you, you'd see everything that's *going* to fall into it. You're seeing the whole history of this point in the universe, from the Big Bang all the way into the faraway future. What's more, the bending of the light rays falling in with you means that you might even be able to see the back of your own head! This is helpful if you want to fix your hair as you prepare for a gruesome death.

Because here's what's happening next: Your feet are closer than your head is to the "singularity" at the black hole's center, so the gravitational pull on them will begin to get much, much stronger. So strong, in fact, that your feet will get pulled away from your head at hundreds of millions of times the gravity on Earth, stretching you out like taffy. This process is called *spaghettification*, because scientists are gross, and also they really like Italian food.

What happens at the singularity? Nobody knows. Science-fiction writers love the theory that black holes might be tunnels into another universe altogether, where all the light and radiation they absorbed emerges from "white hole" exits. But there's no evidence for this yet, and anyway, you won't care in your new spaghetti-shaped self.

Extra Credit

The energy sprayed out by a black hole can literally smash hydrogen and oxygen atoms together—to make water! Astronomers studying a black hole 12 billion light-years away from Earth have discovered that it's surrounded by a cloud of water so massive that it could supply twenty-eight galaxies! This space reservoir contains 20,000 *planets'* worth of water— oceans, rivers, glaciers, wading pools—for every single man, woman, and child on Earth!

Solid Gold

Voyager packed along one very unusual item when it was launched. A record album! Luckily—even though it was pressed in 1977—it wasn't disco music. This two-hour gold record was designed

as a short introduction to life on Earth for anyone who happened to encounter *Voyager* on its travels.

The astronomer Carl Sagan, who produced the record, said he was "launching [a] bottle into the cosmic ocean. . . ." The record jacket includes instructions on how to play the disk, in case alien races don't have a record player handy, and on the record are encoded:

115 photographs of life on Earth

A selection of people saying "Hello" in fifty-five different languages

Recordings of birdsong, whalesong, and other natural Earth sounds

Music recordings, from Beethoven to Mozart to rock-and-roll pioneer Chuck Berry

Extra Credit

Unlike the earlier *Pioneer* probe, the record jacket does *not* contain a picture of human beings. NASA received many complaints from taxpayers who were angry that the couple drawn on *Pioneer* were naked!

A Whole New World

The odds are very low that an alien life form is grooving to the *Voyager* record right now. But the odds are actually pretty good that we are not alone in the universe. After all, there are 400 billion stars in the Milky Way galaxy alone. As recently as the early 1990s, astronomers couldn't be sure that planets orbited any of these other suns, but we've now discovered over a thousand *exoplanets*. Most of them don't sound like fun places to grow up.

51 PEGASI B is so close to its sun that its metallic surface vaporizes into the atmosphere, allowing iron clouds to rain molten metal on you.

HD 189733B has winds whipping across its surface at over six times the speed of sound. Don't bring a Frisbee.

KEPLER-7B hurtles around its sun so fast that a year there only lasts eight hours!

COROT-3B is the size of a small star and denser than lead. You'd feel like an elephant was sitting on you.

OGLE-2005-BLG-390LB has a climate that's even worse than its not-very-catchy name. The average temperature is -370 degrees Fahrenheit on this desolate ice ball.

But with new telescopes we can also see hundreds of exoplanets that seem to lie within their solar systems' habitable Goldilocks zone. There could be 60 billion of these habitable planets in our galaxy!

E.T. Phone Home

In 1961 an astronomer named Frank Drake created this equation: $N = R* \cdot f_p \cdot n_e \cdot f_l \cdot f_i \cdot f_c \cdot L$

It looks complicated, but it's really just a way to guess how many advanced alien races might be out there. Depending on how you choose the inputs, the Drake Equation estimates that N, the number of alien civilizations in our galaxy, might even be in the millions.

Extra Credit

Have any of these civilizations ever visited Earth? Thousands of people over the years have reported contact with UFOs—unidentified flying objects—but none have ever proved to be an actual "flying saucer." Think about this: Thanks to the invention of the smartphone, millions of us always have good-quality cameras in our pockets. If people are really meeting aliens all the time, why haven't we seen pictures yet?

NO PICTURES, PLEASE!

But many people still insist that UFOs are real. One British insurance firm has sold more than thirty thousand policies that include "alien abduction insurance"! You can't be too careful, I guess.

Dr. Drake was also one of the founders of SETI, which stands for Search for Extraterrestrial Intelligence. SETI researchers use radio telescopes to scan the stars, hoping to find evidence of signals from another world.

In 1977, at Ohio State University, the astronomer Jerry R. Ehman heard a signal from the direction of the constellation Sagittarius that was so intense and unexpected that he wrote "Wow!" in the margin of the printout. Astronomers have been unable to explain or replicate the so-called Wow! signal, but they're still listening.

War of the Worlds

Not all scientists think that searching for extraterrestrial life is a good idea. Stephen Hawking says that, in his opinion, there's too great a risk that the alien races who notice Earth would decide to "conquer and colonize" us!

The biggest question in SETI research today is this: If our galaxy could be home to millions of civilizations, why haven't we heard from them yet? This problem is

called the Fermi Paradox, aka "Where is everybody?" Could the aliens be hiding from us? Could they be too far away? Could a habitable planet like Earth be much, much rarer than we think? Do advanced civilizations tend to get wiped out before they can explore much? It's one of the most puzzling mysteries of the universe.

To Infinity . . . and Beyond!

Voyager will spend billions and billions of years orbiting our galaxy, which is over 100,000 light-years across. There's plenty to see. But the Milky Way is just one galaxy in our cosmic neighborhood—a cluster of about fifty nearby galaxies that we call the Local Group. And even the Local Group, as vast as it is, is a *teeny, tiny* part of the known universe, which contains as many as 500 billion galaxies! These galaxies come in all different sizes and shapes.

If you want to visit another galaxy, I would recommend our nearest neighbor, M31, also known as the Andromeda Galaxy. You won't even need a spaceship! In 4 billion years, the Andromeda Galaxy is due to collide with the Milky Way. We're currently hurtling toward it at more than sixty miles a second.

In general, though, most things in space are getting farther away from us. That's because the universe is constantly expanding. In fact, some scientists think that it's accelerating, with stuff moving *away from us faster and faster all the time!*

As a professional collector of great knowledge, it makes me very sad that we here on Earth will never know *anything* about most of the universe. Why? Because it's impossible to observe. It's been about 13.8 billion years since the Big Bang that created the universe. Light from *most* of the galaxies in our universe hasn't had time to get to us yet! We are stuck with only ever being able to see a small portion of what's out there.

Is the universe finite, or does it literally go on forever, in all directions? We don't know. If the universe really is infinite, then it's possible that there are an infinite number of versions of you out there on distant planets. Some of them might be reading a book very much like this one!

Who knows? If we ever figure out faster-than-light travel, we may someday finally get to see parts of the *uno*bservable universe. If you ever find a version of me on an alien planet somewhere, please say "Hi" to myself for me.

SEVENTH PERIOD

The Final Frontier

On April 12, 1961, a forest ranger's wife named Anna Takhtarova and her granddaughter Rita were weeding potatoes outside the tiny village of Smelovka, in southwestern Russia. They were amazed to see a figure in a bright orange suit and a big white helmet fall from the sky with a parachute and walk across the field toward them. "Don't be afraid!" he called. "I am a Soviet citizen like you!" Then he asked if there was a telephone he could use to call Moscow. This was Russian pilot Yuri Gagarin, and two hours earlier he had just become the first human being in space.

It's been over fifty years since *Vostok 1*, Gagarin's tiny capsule, orbited the Earth. Since then, more than five hundred people have followed his footsteps into

space. But remember that 10 billion people or so have lived on Earth since 1961, so if you were a resident of Earth during the last half century (and I have to assume that you were, Junior Geniuses!) your odds of being an astronaut were something like one in 20 million. You're much more likely to be attacked by a shark, or give birth to identical quadruplets.

Traffic Jam

The largest number of people who have ever been in space at one time? Just thirteen. This first happened in 1995, when a Russian Soyuz mission and the space shuttle *Endeavour* were both in orbit at the same time, while three cosmonauts circled the Earth on the *Mir* space station.

But don't despair. In your lifetime, I predict that you will see amazing things happen in space exploration: moon bases, asteroid capturing, Mars missions . . . who knows? If you dream of going to space like I did when I was your age . . . well, I'd say your odds are much better than mine.

Today we're going to learn what life is like for men and women in space, so that you're all ready to go when your launch date arrives.

Life in a Tin Can

There's no up or down in space, but space travel does have its upsides and its downsides. Not everything about exploring the universe is as glamorous as it might seem in the movies. Astronauts spend a *lot* more time consulting mission checklists than they do fighting laser battles. In the 1960s, at least they got a free Corvette when they landed back on Earth. But those days are done.

Just so you know what you're getting yourself into, future astronauts, here's a sneak preview of the best and worst parts of space travel.

 WEIGHTLESSNESS! Contrary to popular belief, the gravitational pull on a person in orbit is almost the same as it is on Earth. So why do astronauts feel weightless? For the same reason you feel weightless when a roller coaster plunges straight down: Astronauts, like their spacecraft, are constantly falling. That's what an orbit is: You're constantly falling toward the ground, but you're also moving forward fast

enough (17,500 miles per hour or so!) that instead of smashing into the Earth, you just keep falling *around* it in a curve.

MOTION SICKNESS. The downside of weightlessness is that the human tummy wasn't designed for changes in g-forces, so about two-thirds of all astronauts get "space-sick." *Apollo 9* crew member Rusty Schweickart

barfed *twice*, almost canceling a planned space walk. (Throwing up in weightlessness is no fun, but losing your lunch inside a spacesuit is, as you can probably imagine, *really* bad news.) In 1985, when Senator Jake Garn went to space, he got so sick that NASA now measures motion sickness on the "Garn scale." If an astronaut gets up to ten Garns, that's as miserable as he or she can be.

THE SIGHTS! Aboard the International Space Station you'll enjoy sixteen sunrises and sixteen sunsets a day! That's one every forty-five minutes.

THE SMELLS. If you don't like having to take a bath, space is the place for you! NASA has experimented with space showers, but the little water droplets just float everywhere, and you can even choke on them. So today's astronauts stay clean with disposable wipes. Many buzz their hair so they don't need to worry about shampoo.

SEE ATOMS! Outside of Earth's magnetic field, astronauts get pummeled by atomic particles called cosmic rays. The cool part is that when these rays pass through astronauts' eyeballs, they can actually see them, as white spots or streaks making flashes in their field of vision.

GET ZAPPED. The downside of these cosmic rays is they're so intense that astronauts get classified as radiation workers. We're still not sure what the long-term effects of exposure to space rays are.

 **GET TALLER!** NASA makes sure its spacesuits are sized up, because most people get around two inches taller after liftoff! It's a result of weightlessness stretching out the spine.

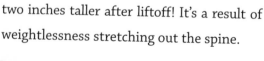

GET WEAKER. Unfortunately, you'll also start to lose bone mass in space—1 to 2 percent for every month spent in weightlessness. That's the same amount an elderly person might lose in a *year*, so astronauts have to exercise every day to stay healthy. In 2007 Sunita Williams celebrated the Boston Marathon by running a full 26.2-mile marathon aboard the International Space Station—on a treadmill, of course.

LOOK YOUNGER! Without gravity pulling blood downward on your body, your legs start to shrivel and your face bloats up. It's a great way to fight wrinkles!

ACT DUMBER. Due to sleep deprivation, busy schedules, and the other stresses of going to space, astronauts never perform as well in space as they did on the ground. Mission Control calls this the "space stupids."

To Boldly Go . . .

One of the biggest hassles of space travel is something that's so easy on Earth you don't even think about it much: going to the bathroom.

Space toilets have much narrower openings than the ones you're used to. To learn how to poop in space, astronauts train for weeks with simulator toilets that have a camera in the bowl, so they can watch how their, um, approach vector is lining up.

18"

REGULAR TOILET

SPACE TOILET

4"

The shuttle toilet used to grind up waste with razor-sharp blender blades, but astronauts found that this would release clouds of poop dust (yuck!) into the air. The Gemini and Apollo astronauts had it worst of all: They had to use plastic bags, like dogs out for a walk! On *Gemini 7*, Frank Borman's urine bag broke . . . in zero gravity. It was "like spending two weeks in a latrine," his crewmate Jim Lovell remembered.

N O O O O O O O O O O O O O O !

Fur All Mankind

If you wanted to be a space traveler in the 1950s, there was one main qualification.

That's right—the very first space explorers were animals. The United States launched mice and monkeys. The Soviets preferred dogs, because they were calmer and easier to dress. The first living thing to orbit the Earth was a stray dog from the streets of Moscow named Laika ("Barker"). In honor of the Soviet satellite *Sputnik*, the American papers called Laika "Muttnik." Outside St. Petersburg, you can still visit a "Tomb of the Unknown Dog" honoring all the Russian astro-dogs who made human space travel possible.

Extra Credit

In 1961 Soviet premier Nikita Khrushchev presented President Kennedy's family with Pushinka, a puppy that had been born to Strelka ("Arrow"), the second Russian space dog. The CIA X-rayed Pushinka carefully, to make sure she hadn't been implanted with a bug or a bomb!

By 1960 America already had seven astronauts training in its Mercury program: **Alan Shepard, Wally Schirra, Gus Grissom, Gordon Cooper, John Glenn, Deke Slayton,** and **Scott Carpenter.**

But Gagarin beat all of them into space, in part because the United States insisted on animal tests before it would send humans into orbit. Instead of steely-eyed test pilots, the first American astronauts were these handsome heroes:

HAM

ENOS

Ham was named for his laboratory home, the

Holloman

Aerospace

Medical Center. After his flight he retired to a long and happy life in Washington, DC's National Zoo.

Junior Genius Joviality!

Ham was such a celebrity that when President Kennedy's daughter, Caroline, met space hero John Glenn, her only question was:

WHERE'S THE MONKEY?

Today, when we want to study certain science stuff in space, we still send up animals, from frogs to jellyfish to rats to cockroaches. We now know that:

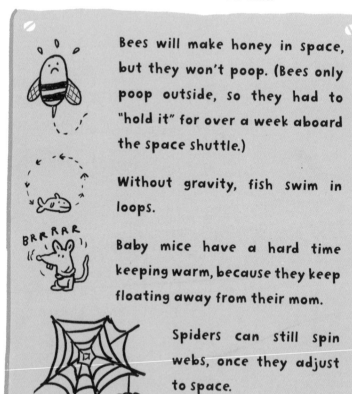

Bees will make honey in space, but they won't poop. (Bees only poop outside, so they had to "hold it" for over a week aboard the space shuttle.)

Without gravity, fish swim in loops.

Baby mice have a hard time keeping warm, because they keep floating away from their mom.

Spiders can still spin webs, once they adjust to space.

Here on Earth, birds can fly, but they won't be flying into space anytime soon. It turns out that most of our feathered friends need gravity to swallow.

Space Oddity

Bugs and rodents aren't the only odd things that get packed along into space. Here are some other odd things that have left Earth's atmosphere.

• **LEGO Minifigures.** NASA's *Juno* probe to Jupiter included LEGO figures representing the astronomer Galileo, and the Roman gods Juno and Jupiter.

• **Salami Pizza.** Pizza Hut delivered a small, thin-crust pie to the International Space Station in 2001 aboard a Russian rocket, at a cost of $1 million. Why salami? Pepperoni doesn't vacuum-seal well, it turns out.

• **Eli Manning's Super Bowl Jersey.** The Giants quarterback offered his helmet as well, but it didn't fit aboard space shuttle *Discovery*.

• **Handguns.** Russian cosmonauts have been packing heat in orbit ever since Yuri Gagarin's day—in case of a bear attack at their landing site.

• **Bird Droppings.** In 2006 NASA noticed that some bird droppings on the wings of *Discovery* had survived a week in space. No wonder you can't get that stuff off your car!

• **Luke Skywalker's Lightsaber.** The original Jedi weapon from *Return of the Jedi* flew to the International Space Station in 2007, to celebrate the thirtieth anniversary of *Star Wars*.

- **Scotty's Ashes.** Actor James Doohan, from *Star Trek*, wanted his remains to go to space when he died. In 2012 a SpaceX rocket finally beamed him up.

- **Stephen Colbert's DNA.** In 2008 the International Space Station installed an "Immortality Drive"—a chip containing the DNA of people like the physicist Stephen Hawking and comedian Stephen Colbert. If something goes terribly wrong on Earth, we now have a backup for the species. We can clone billions of baby Stephen Colberts.

Space Base

Space is no longer just a place we visit, Junior Geniuses. Since October 2000 there has been a continuous human presence 230 miles above the Earth's surface, here:

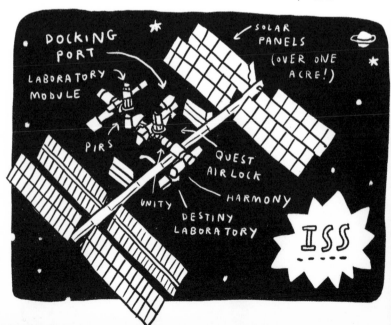

Homework

The size of an entire football field, the International Space Station is the biggest satellite ever placed in orbit—so big you can see it with the naked eye. In fact, there's a NASA phone app that will text or e-mail you every time the station travels overhead, so you can head outside and watch it passing over.

Thanks to the ISS, it's now possible for people to spend years in outer space. The record holder at the moment is Sergei Krikalev, a retired cosmonaut who spent 803 days of his life—over two years—on a series of spaceflights.

The ISS isn't the first manned space station to orbit the Earth—it's the ninth! The Russian Salyut stations and the American *Skylab* were launched in the

1970s. These older stations all crashed to Earth decades ago when their orbits started to decay. *Skylab* scattered debris across Australia as it burned up, and the Australian town of Esperance issued NASA a four-hundred-dollar fine—for littering! When the 150-ton

Russian space station *Mir* fell to Earth in 2001, Taco Bell placed a huge floating target in the South Pacific. If *Mir* had hit the target, every single American would have received a free taco! Tragically, *Mir* splashed down thousands of miles away.

Extra Credit

It's actually a good thing that satellites fall to Earth when we're done with them. To avoid collisions, scientists carefully track the "space junk" that circles the Earth every day—there are over nineteen thousand bits of debris over two inches in size up there, and hundreds of thousands of smaller pieces. The real nightmare scenario is something called the Kessler syndrome, a runaway chain reaction where space junk keeps breaking into smaller and smaller pieces, which in turn cause more and more collisions. One cascade like that could make satellites and space travel impossible for centuries!

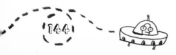

The ISS is the single most expensive object ever built by the human race, at a cost of over $150 *billion*. Why so much? Location, location, location. It costs NASA $10,000 to launch just one pound of payload into orbit! That number has got to get much, much lower if we're going to get serious about exploring our solar system.

The Right Stuff

Sadly, space travel sometimes comes with a human cost as well. When NASA was hiring the first astronauts, they briefly considered hiring acrobats or circus daredevils, but finally settled on test pilots, because they knew they'd keep cool heads in dangerous circumstances.

Make no mistake: Exploring space *is* dangerous. As one NASA engineer pointed out, the Apollo missions each had 5.6 million parts. Even if those parts were all 99.9 percent reliable, there would still be 5,600 failures. Looking back, NASA now knows that the first nine space shuttle flights had a one-in-nine chance of "catastrophic failure." Before he left for the Moon, Neil Armstrong couldn't afford life insurance, but he mailed himself a stack of autographed envelopes, so that his family could sell them off if he never returned from space.

Tragedies from Yuri Gagarin's death in a 1968 training jet all the way through the *Challenger* and *Columbia* shuttle explosions show that space exploration has many, many risks. But it's certainly safer today than it's ever been—and brave astronauts are willing to face its dangers. "We are in a risky business," said Gus Grissom, who died in a fire while training for the first Apollo mission. "The conquest of space is worth the risk of life."

Reaching for the Stars

If space travel is so expensive and so dangerous, why do it? Well, for one thing, because space research makes life better for everyone. It's estimated that every one dollar NASA spends on space adds about eight dollars to the U.S. economy. Here are a few of the many, many inventions that we only get to use on Earth because of research for space:

MEMORY FOAM IN MATTRESSES

UV-BLOCKING SUNGLASSES

NITINOL, THE METAL BRACES ARE MADE OUT OF

SATELLITE TV

MORE NUTRITIOUS BABY FOOD

But the real reason we go to space has nothing to do with water guns or basketball shoes. We dream of space because exploration has always been important to the human spirit. We will always want to see things we have never seen and do things that have never been done.

In a 1962 speech about the Apollo program, President Kennedy said:

"We choose to go to the Moon. We choose to go to the Moon in this decade and do the other things, not because they are easy, but because they are hard, because that goal will serve to organize and measure the best of our energies and skills, because that challenge is one that we are willing to accept, one we are unwilling to postpone, and one which we intend to win. . . ."

ARTIFICIAL LIMBS

ATHLETIC SHOES

WATER GUNS

FOREST FIRE DETECTION

HOME BLOOD-PRESSURE KITS

If you are willing to accept the challenge of space, Junior Geniuses, then it will take the best of your energies and skills. Maybe someday when I'm old I'll pick up a holographic digital newspaper and see that *you* have just become one of the first human colonists on the Moon or Mars.

We'll never know if we don't try!

OFFICIAL
JUNIOR GENIUS
CERTIFICATION
EXAM

NAME : ―――――――――――――――――

DATE : ―――――――――――――――――

At the beginning of this book, your brain might have been as empty as the vacuum of space, but now it's been so packed full of interplanetary information that it's as dense as a neutron star. Time to grab a number 2 pencil and see if you can certify as an Official Space Junior Genius.

Wait for it.

Wait for it. . . .

BEGIN.

OFFICIAL JUNIOR GENIUS CERTIFICATION EXAM

1. Polaris is the star in our sky closest to what?

Ⓐ The Andromeda Galaxy
Ⓑ Due north
Ⓒ The horizon
Ⓓ Earth

2. What happened when a protoplanet called Theia struck the Earth?

Ⓐ The dinosaurs died.
Ⓑ The asteroid belt was born.
Ⓒ The Moon formed.
Ⓓ Earth entered the "Goldilocks zon

3. What do scientists plot on a Hertzsprung-Russell diagram?

Ⓐ Comets
Ⓑ Planets
Ⓒ Stars
Ⓓ Galaxies

4. What Martian peak is over fourteen miles high?

Ⓐ Rheasilvia
Ⓑ Mare Tranquillitatus
Ⓒ Caloris Basin
Ⓓ Olympus Mons

5. Like other stars, the Sun is a giant furnace fusing hydrogen into what?

Ⓐ Oxygen
Ⓑ Carbon
Ⓒ Nitrogen
Ⓓ Helium

6. Who was the first human being in space?

Ⓐ Alan Shepard   Ⓑ John Glenn

Ⓒ Neil Armstrong   Ⓓ Yuri Gagarin

7. Twenty-three percent of the universe is made of what mysterious substance?

Ⓐ Plasma   Ⓑ Cosmic background radiation

Ⓒ Dark matter   Ⓓ Chocolate

8. What is the hottest planet in the solar system?

Ⓐ Mercury   Ⓑ Venus

Ⓒ Earth   Ⓓ Mars

9. What animals have trouble swallowing in space?

Ⓐ Fish   Ⓑ Birds

Ⓒ Rodents   Ⓓ Insects

10. What color is the storm on Jupiter that's as large as three Earths?

Ⓐ Blue   Ⓑ White

Ⓒ Green   Ⓓ Red

11. Meteor showers like the Perseids are caused by the Earth passing through what?

Ⓐ A comet's tail

Ⓑ The Kuiper Belt

Ⓒ The Moon's shadow

Ⓓ The ecliptic

12. The Drake Equation and Fermi Paradox refer to the problem of finding what in space?

Ⓐ Intelligent life

Ⓑ Black holes

Ⓒ Supernovas

Ⓓ Other galaxies

13. You find a tiny chunk of space rock on Earth. What is it called?

Ⓐ A meteor

Ⓑ A meteoroid

Ⓒ A meteorite

Ⓓ Gary

14. Pluto and the other "trans-Neptunian objects" are now classified as what?

Ⓐ Dwarf planets

Ⓑ Exoplanets

Ⓒ Failed planets

Ⓓ Planetoids

15. When can we see the Sun's corona?

Ⓐ During solar flares

Ⓑ At the solstices

Ⓒ Sunrise and sunset

Ⓓ During eclipses

16. Which of these things does *not* happen to the average astronaut?

Ⓐ They get motion sickness.

Ⓑ They get shorter.

Ⓒ They lose bone mass.

Ⓓ They see cosmic rays.

17. What kind of satellite is the Hubble, put in orbit in 1990?

Ⓐ Space telescope

Ⓑ Space station

Ⓒ Weather satellite

Ⓓ Jupiter probe

18. Mercury and Venus are the only planets without what?

Ⓐ Atmospheres

Ⓑ Moons

Ⓒ Rings

Ⓓ Volcanic activity

19. What objects in space are surrounded by event horizons?

Ⓐ Black holes

Ⓑ Spiral galaxies

Ⓒ Pulsars

Ⓓ Gas giants

20. Which of these sports has been played on the Moon?

Ⓐ Badminton

Ⓑ Baseball

Ⓒ Golf

Ⓓ Water polo

Time's up, pencils down! Check your answers on the next page.

ANSWERS

1.	2.	3.	4.	5.
6.	7.	8.	9.	10.
11.	12.	13.	14.	15.
16.	17.	18.	19.	20.

SCORING

16–20	Certified Junior Genius!
13–15	At the Event Horizon
10–12	AstroNaut-Too-Shabby
6–9	Houston, We Have a Problem
0–5	Failure to Launch

If you achieved escape velocity on your first flight, congratulations! I have your official certificate all ready to go at JuniorGeniusGuides.com.

But don't get discouraged if you spaced out. Being a Junior Genius is like being an astronomer or astronaut: It means never giving up on the pursuit of knowledge. You can take the test as many times as you need to pass. It's like the Romans used to say: *"Per aspera ad astra!"* Through hardships to the stars!

HOMEWORK

If your excitement about space is as unlimited as the universe itself, here are some projects that will let you continue your mission even after our class is over for the day.

○ **Design a space colony.** What do you think a permanent human colony on the Moon or Mars would look like? Use the medium of your choice (pencil and paper, LEGO bricks, Minecraft) to imagine one. Give some thought to the BIG problems of living on a lifeless world. How do the colonists breathe? Where does their power come from? Where is the closest good pizza place?

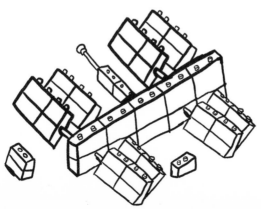

○ **Try weightlessness.** When NASA astronauts need to train in microgravity, they board a special jet-liner and take to the sky. By suddenly dropping the plane ten thousand feet or so, the pilot can simulate almost thirty seconds of weightlessness at a time. The experience is so unpleasant that astronauts call the plane the "Vomit Comet." If you don't have your own jetliner at home, simulate weightlessness by standing in a doorway and pressing the backs of your hands against the door frame for thirty seconds or so. (If a doorway is too wide, try two chairs.) Step away and relax your arms. They'll float up on their own, just like you're in orbit!

○ **Tour the Moon.** Even through a small telescope or binoculars, there's a lot to see on the Moon. Print out a Moon map that shows some of the easier features to spot and head outside on a moonlit night. You might be able to find craters like Copernicus and Aristarchus (they'll be bright) or Grimaldi (it'll be dark) as well as

maria like the Sea of Serenity, the Sea of Moisture, and especially the Sea of Tranquility, where Neil Armstrong and Buzz Aldrin went for a stroll. Don't worry if there's not a full Moon out—you'll actually see more detail along the terminator than anywhere else.

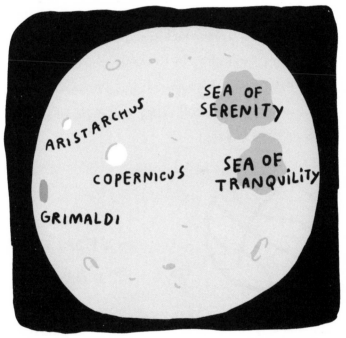

o **Shrink the solar system.** Find someplace you can walk in a more-or-less-straight line for half a mile—a pasture, maybe, or a trail in a park. As you walk, make a miniature solar system like the one we imagined in a baseball diamond earlier. Make the sun a basketball.

Place a pinhead for Mercury in the ground twelve yards away, then two small peas (Venus and Earth) twenty-two and thirty-one yards away from the basketball. For Mars, place a peppercorn forty-seven yards away. Jupiter can be a Ping-Pong ball 162 yards away, and Saturn something slightly smaller (a Super Ball or oversized marble) 297 yards away. Uranus and Neptune are small marbles 598 and 937 yards away. By this time, you'll probably be too tired to represent our nearest star, Proxima Centauri, with a second basketball. That would mean another 4,300 miles of walking!

THE FINAL BELL

Let's go from the telescope to the microscope! Can you point to . . .

○ the one bone in your body that's not attached to any other bone?

○ the part of your body that can dissolve razor blades?

○ the part of your body whose tiny muscles move 100,000 times per day?

The next Junior Genius Guide will explore the miracle of the amazing human body. I expect to see all *your* bodies here in your seats bright and early, or you're going to miss out on a lot of cool facts, and also some gross ones. Do you know how many bathtubs full of saliva your mouth can produce in a lifetime? Hint: *more than one.*

Until then, my friends, always live by the Junior Genius Slogan. In the words of the great thinker Blaise Pascal: "It is much better to know something about everything than everything about something."

Class dismissed!

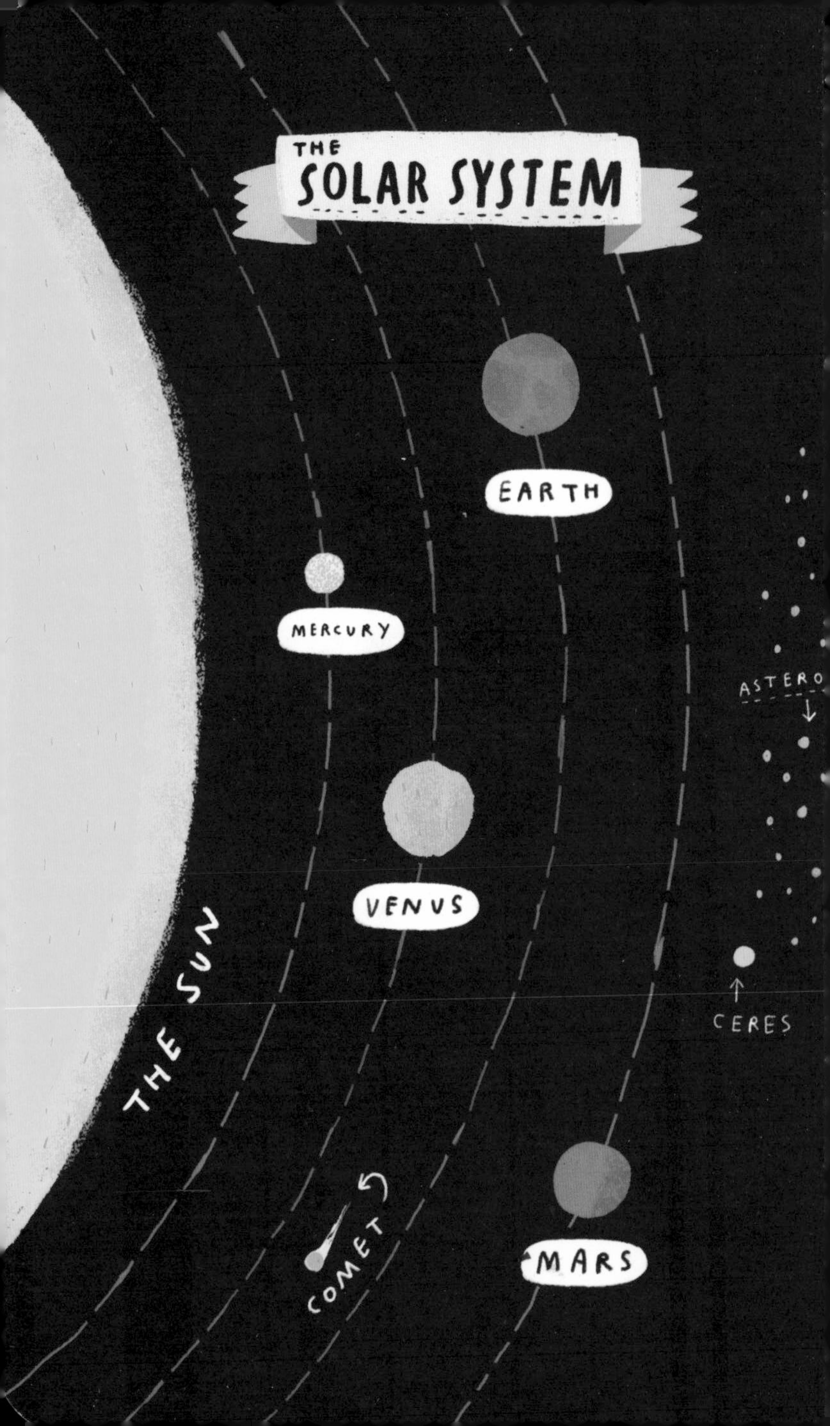

THE
SOLAR SYSTEM

EARTH

MERCURY

ASTERO
↓

VENUS

CERES
↑

THE SUN

COMET

MARS